"Jesus said that His faithful stewards would bring out of their storehouses things both old and new. Gill does precisely that in this book. You will find familiar characters and their well-known stories, but just as you think you know what is coming, the text surprises you with fresh insights that make you see these narratives in a new way." - **David Faulkner, Presbyter, East Solent and Downs Methodist Circuit**

AS TOLD BY

**Bible Stories by Those
Who Were There**

Copyright © 2024 Gill Taggart

The moral right of the author has been asserted.

Apart from any fair dealing for the purposes of research or private study, or criticism or re-view, as permitted under Copyright, Design and Patents Act 1998, this publication may only be reproduced, stored or transmitted, in any form or by any means, with prior permission in writing of the publishers, or in any case of the reprographic reproduction in accordance with the terms of licences issued by the Copyright Licensing Agency. Enquiries concerning repro-duction outside these terms should be sent to the publishers.

PublishU Ltd

www.PublishU.com

Scripture from the Holy Bible, New International Version®, NIV®.

Copyright © 1973, 1978, 1984, 2011 by Biblica, Inc.™ Used by permission of Zondervan. All rights reserved worldwide.

All rights of this publication are reserved.

AS TOLD BY

Contents

Introduction

Chapter 1   The Pair on the Ground

Chapter 2   The Nonagenarian Father

Chapter 3   The Scammer

Chapter 4   Arguing with God

Chapter 5   The Widows

Chapter 6   The Adulterous King

Chapter 7   The Fire-Starter

Chapter 8   The Locust Muncher

Chapter 9   A Special Calling

Chapter 10   The Forgotten Ones

Chapter 11   The Son of Thunder

Chapter 12   The Jesus Hater

Conclusion

About the Author

Notes

GILL TAGGART

AS TOLD BY

Introduction

I have always enjoyed creative writing, and I have almost always enjoyed reading the Bible, but they are not two activities that I would have thought of putting together. So imagine my surprise when I was introduced to the "personalised narrative sermon" while training as a preacher. This involves re-telling a Bible story from the viewpoint of one of the characters involved; putting yourself into the scene.

Despite the word "sermon", I believe that it's something that anyone can try. Read the parable of the Prodigal Son and re-tell it from the father's point of view, for example. What might he have thought; how might he have felt?

I have used this method several times over the years and have found it to be effective and powerful. It gave me a new perspective and, I'm told, my listeners thought so too.

This book aims to bring the Bible to life for those who might not otherwise want to read it. I have chosen fifteen characters who tell their own stories. This, inevitably, involves some poetic licence. I appreciate some may not like this approach but, if the Bible is silent on a subject; i.e. people's reactions, how their decisions affect them or how they feel about the things that happened to them, it is surely not wrong to use our imaginations. I have heard this referred to as "sanctified imagination."

In other places, I have closely followed the Biblical narrative, and quoted from it where appropriate.

I hope you enjoy this book.

AS TOLD BY

Chapter 1
The Pair on the Ground[1]
As Told by Adam and Eve

Adam

My name is Adam and I live in paradise (I don't know if it's really called that, but it feels as though it should be). It's beautiful here; a perfect garden. Many of the trees are covered in delicate, lightly scented blossom, and produce all kinds of mouth-watering fruit. Squirrels scamper up and down their trunks and other creatures hide in, perch or swing from their branches. A river provides us with water. Rabbits frisk on its flower-strewn banks, fish swim in the crystal waters and, further along, other rivers wend their way into distant lands. Most evenings a fiery sunset blazes across the sky, slowly turning to inky black. Sometimes soft rain waters the ground; occasionally thunder may boom forth while vivid lightning crackles across the sky. There are many kinds of creatures in this paradise: those that fly, those that swim and others that walk on the land. Some have feathers, some have fur, skin or scales. The One who made me gave me the task of naming them all. That was fun, but it took a while, I can tell you! It's so blissful and peaceful I could be happy here forever. At least, that's what I thought.

I had been there for several days – or maybe weeks, or months – when, one day, a strange thought flitted across my mind, "Is this all there is?" I know that sounds incredibly ungrateful. I was surrounded by beauty. I had as much food as I wanted, the freedom to go where I pleased, and the antics and habits of numerous creatures to keep me company. But I was on my own. No creature looked like me and, though I talked often with the One who made me, the conversation was somewhat limited. The One who made me must have thought so too, because He observed that it wasn't good for me to be alone, without a helper. He put me into a deep sleep and, when I awoke, there was another creature beside me. She had been made from one of my ribs. She wasn't exactly like me; she was stunning.

I had been told that I was not to eat fruit from the tree of good and evil, or I would surely die. But one day, the woman came to me holding a fruit from that tree out for me to try. I froze. She had picked the forbidden fruit! We weren't supposed to do that. She would surely die now. She had picked fruit for both of us though and had almost eaten hers and said that it was delicious. Not only was she still alive, but she was also as stunning as ever – though, was that a small blemish that I saw on her nose? The fruit looked good and I wondered how something so perfect, made by the One who had made us, could bring death. So I ate some. It was exquisite. Yet, it seemed to turn bitter in my stomach as I suddenly realised what I had done. I had specifically been told, by the One who made me, that I could eat fruit from any tree in the Garden, except one. But I had just eaten fruit from that tree. I think my wife must have had the same thought, for we looked at each other in horror and shame for our nakedness. Then we plaited some leaves together to cover ourselves up and we hid. The One who made us was walking in the Garden, calling us by name. I didn't want to see Him; I was sure that "guilty" was written all over my face. But the One who made me asked where we were, why we had hidden from Him and what we had done.

We stepped out from behind the bush and I told Him,

> *"The woman You put here with me, she gave me some fruit...and I ate it"* (Genesis 3:12).

I think I said that last bit rather quickly, but it was true. He had given the woman to me, and she had given me the fruit. He asked my wife the same question and I noticed that she blamed the serpent for tricking her. Well, that was true as well – he started it. But though we had done wrong, the One who made us had also been economical with the truth. We hadn't died, as He'd said we would.

I turned my head away and caught sight of my reflection in one of the crystal clear streams. Was that a wrinkle on my forehead, fear in my eyes and a tightening of my mouth? The One who made me didn't seem to have noticed. Then He began to speak, like a judge passing a sentence. He told the serpent that from that moment onwards it was an accursed creature. The serpent, who had been so proud of its beauty and the ease with which it tricked these humans, would crawl on its belly all its days. It would be feared and hated by the ones it had deceived; for now. But one day one of our descendants would bruise its head; overcome and defeat it. The One who made me told both of us that, although we would be fruitful, it would be more difficult. My wife would bring new humans into the world, but that beautiful act would be accompanied by great pain. At the same time, I would suffer pain in coaxing the land into producing food for us. Briars and thorns would spring up in the garden; choking new life and sapping its resources. I had been created from the soil of the earth and, one day, I would return to it.

And it was so. My wife (to whom I gave the name, "Eve") and I were escorted from the Garden. Had we stayed and eaten from the Tree of Life, we would have lived forever – in pain, guilt and sin.

We had our first son, Cain, who worked on the land and tilled the soil. Later we had a second son, Abel, who became a shepherd. These fine boys also caused us pain, I'm sorry to say. Cain was jealous of his brother, saw something that he wanted – God's approval – and decided to kill Abel to try to get it. After that, we had another son, whom we named Seth. By this time, Cain was in the land of Nod. No, he wasn't asleep; Nod was where he lived. He had a son of his own, called Enoch. In time, our lad Seth grew up and also had a child of his own, called Enosh.

And that is my story. We had everything and we lost it. I have to accept responsibility for disobeying the

One who made me. I had heard Him tell me not to do something, yet I did it. My disobedience, or bad decision, has followed me for the whole of my life.
Though the One who made me never left, or gave up on me, that act of disobedience changed our relationship for good; it was almost as though something had died.

I hope that one day someone might be able to reverse that mistake.

Eve

I can't say that I was born, exactly. But I came from Eden. That is to say, I lived there for a while. I came from one of my husband's ribs, which may sound a little bizarre, but it's what happened. Despite that, I was made by Someone and for a purpose. I was also made in His image. That might sound bizarre also; I don't mean that I look exactly like the One who made me, nor He like me. But something of His nature — His character — is also in me. I imagine it's a bit like when I had my boys. Cain looks very much like me and maybe has my impulsive nature. Abel was the image of my husband and shared his interests. It's fitting that Adam named the animals, and his son looked after them. I can see both our features in Seth, though he, too, has my husband's nature. The point is that the One who made this garden, the sky, the sun and so on from nothing, also made us and in some way, we are like Him.

It seems that before I arrived, the One who made us

gave my husband a command: not to eat fruit from a certain tree. This information was passed on to me, but I dare say that I wasn't listening properly. The Garden was so beautiful and there was always something that caught my attention. After some time, one of the creatures, a serpent, came up to me and asked me if we really were not allowed to eat fruit from this particular tree. I suppose I should have asked him why he needed to know, but I replied that we were not to eat it or even touch it, otherwise we would die.

"You won't die," said the creature, who was rather beautiful to look at and almost hypnotic.

> *"God knows that when you eat from it, your eyes will be opened, and you will be like God"* (Genesis 3:5).

I hesitated. I was fairly sure Adam had warned me not to do this. But I did want to be like the One who made me; good and kind (By that time, I had already forgotten that I was made in His image.). I took a bite.

The fruit was delicious at first; tangy, refreshing and not too sweet and I gave some to my husband.

I think we realised, at about the same time, what we had done. The fruit seemed to turn bitter in my stomach, making me feel sick. The creature who had enticed me to eat scurried away, with a rather triumphant look on its face. And we could only run and hide as we heard the One who made us walk in the garden.

He must have been able to see the two of us, yet He called out and asked us where we were. Adam said later that He didn't need to know that, but that He instead was asking us to come out into the open; to be honest about what we had done.

I began to feel emotions that I had not felt before a kind of fearful embarrassment and a desire to hurt the creature who had tricked me and placed me in this position. "The serpent deceived me," I told the One who made me, "That's why I ate it." It was true, after all. Or partly; I didn't have to listen. Anyway, Adam was trying to put all the blame onto me, which made me angry. Well yes, I had listened to the serpent and let him talk me into doing something which I had felt was wrong. But I wasn't completely sure what Adam had been told and I didn't know our Maker very well. Surely Adam could have corrected me or helped me to understand?

The One who made all things told the serpent that there would be mistrust, even fear, between it and humans. But one day, a human would crush it and destroy its power. I'm not sure what that meant, but it sounded as though, one day, one of my descendants would punish this creature who had tricked me. Well, good; why should it be let off? But I wasn't going to get an easy ride either. My decision to listen to the serpent rather than God had been a foolish one. I had offered Adam the fruit that we were not allowed to eat (though I didn't make him take it). When I was created, I was taken from Adam's side. We were equals; equally made in the image of our Maker. But from then onward he would be the head of our relationship. From then on, too, the act of bringing new humans into the world was going to bring me pain.

And it was so. In time, with God's help, I gave birth to our first son, Cain. Later on, we had Abel. Their entries into the world caused me great physical pain, just as I had been told they would. But that was nothing compared to the pain I felt when, some years later, Cain killed his brother. It seems that both wanted to offer sacrifices to the One who made us. Cain worked on the land, so it was fitting that he should take produce as his sacrifice. Abel looked after the flocks and had taken some of the firstborn animals as his. This latter sacrifice pleased the One who made us and he favoured Abel, which made Cain very angry. He was the eldest. God should have favoured him – his brother didn't need to be so smug about it. I'm not exactly sure what passed between them, but Cain somehow persuaded his brother to go into the field, and there he killed him. Why, Cain? Why would you do such a thing? Why have you deprived your father and me of a son? If offering the wrong sacrifice displeased the One who made you, what will He say now that you have taken your brother's life? How can you put that right?

Cain was driven from the land for doing wrong, just as we had been. His wife gave birth to a son, Enoch. But we never saw them, as Cain became a wanderer on earth, never settling in one place for very long. We had, effectively, lost both sons.

A year or so later, I gave birth to another boy, whom

we called Seth. It was as though God had given him to us in place of Abel; though, of course, no one ever could replace him. Years later, Seth himself took a wife and they welcomed a son into the world.

And that is my story, more or less. I have known great joy and great sorrow in my life. We had everything, yet disobeyed the One who made us and lost it. I had to accept some responsibility for that and, for the rest of my life, I lived with the consequences. Yet the One who made me did not give up on me and gave me a promise of restoration.

I wonder when, and how, that dreadful serpent will be crushed and its power destroyed.

GILL TAGGART

AS TOLD BY

Chapter 2
The Nonagenarian Father
As Told by Abraham

My name is Abraham. It wasn't always though — I was born Abram (but more of that later). My father's name was Terah and my seventeenth great grandfather was Adam. I have two sons; my eldest son has a different mother. I'm afraid that that wasn't one of the finest moments of my life. In my defence, it was all rather complicated. But maybe I had better start from the beginning.

It all started when the One who made me spoke to me. We don't know the name of this God: He doesn't speak to everybody and He often doesn't speak at all. But we know that He created us; in His image, no less! We can have His characteristics, qualities and reflect His character.

He has also given us many blessings — except that Sarai and I didn't have the blessing of children. That was actually quite a big deal for us and Sarai, in particular, had many years of disappointment, heartache and sometimes, teasing from mean-spirited women who considered themselves superior because they had children. As the years went on, we buried our disappointment and got on with our lives.

The One who made me told me that I was to leave my father's household, and even my country, to go somewhere else. I asked where I would be going; a reasonable question, I would have thought. But I was told that I'd know when I got there. He also said that I would become a great nation, be blessed and a blessing to others. I wasn't quite sure what that meant. My name, Abram, means "exulted father." I didn't mind being exulted, but the "father" part was woefully inaccurate and I couldn't see how I could become a nation. But I left my country, along with Sarai, our servants, animals and my nephew – "Lot" and his household. We journeyed for several years, staying in various places. Occasionally our stay was short. The One who made me would sometimes give me a promise or assurance of His presence. Then I would build an altar, worship Him and move on. Sometimes we stayed in a place for quite a bit longer. Our journey was not without drama. On one occasion we went to Egypt to escape a famine and quickly left again after I messed up. I had been afraid that Pharaoh might kill me and take Sarai for his wife, so I told her to say that she was my sister. Pharaoh was angry when he discovered the truth.

It was soon after this that Lot and I decided to part company; we had simply both become very wealthy and the land could not support both of us. Oh yes, even back then we cared about the environment, the land which God had given us to tend. So Lot chose to go in one direction, I went in another and God repeated His promise that He would give that land to me and to my offspring. Don't get me wrong, it was amazing that my Maker should even speak to me, never mind promise me anything; but it was beginning to get a little wearing. There were no offspring. I could see no signs that God was about to fulfil His promise. So why was He saying these things?

Time passed. Life was sometimes challenging; sometimes run of the mill; sometimes good, as life often is. We grew older. There were still no children.

Then the One who made me appeared to me.

That was a shock. I wondered if my latest batch of home-made wine had been a little too strong. He told me not to be afraid; that He was going to protect me and that my reward would be great. Yes, well, I reminded that He had said this before. Yet He had still given me no children. My slave was set to become my heir. That wine must have been strong after all; it was madness to talk like this. But God didn't seem to mind my saying what was in my heart. He took me outside the tent, told me to look into the sky and try to count the stars. "That's how many descendants you will have," He said, "And I will give you possession of this land."

My servant was not to be my heir after all, but I would have a child of my own! Strangely, I believed Him. It did not seem odd that the One who made me and knew me could give me a child – my greatest desire (even if it did seem that age was against us). I did ask for assurance that I would possess the land; all those years of travelling around had taken their toll. God graciously gave me the assurance that I wanted. Sarai didn't have any such reassurance, however, and the burden of not having had any children was harder for her to bear. She had an Egyptian servant called Hagar and had the idea that if Hagar was to give me a son, she would be able to raise him as her own. It was not only our slaves who belonged to us, but their children as well. That sounded reasonable; the One who made me had not told me exactly how He was going to provide me with a son, and this could have been the answer.

Hagar became pregnant. But then she started to treat my lovely wife with contempt: yet another woman thought she was superior because she was with child. Sarai didn't need to be around someone who taunted her physically and verbally about her failure as a woman, so she responded by sending Hagar away. Later, Hagar gave birth to a son and harmony was restored. I thought that would be that; we now had a child, who would grow up and give us grandchildren. We would have descendants, after all. Better late than never.

But that wasn't what God had in mind.

It must have been almost ten years later that He appeared to me once again. This time He told me that He was El Shaddai; Almighty God. After revealing His name to me, God said that He was going to change ours. I would be called Abraham, which means "father of many"; I would have many descendants. This was the covenant that El Shaddai, the One who made me, was making with me. Though I was now living in Canaan as a foreigner, He was going to give the land to me, and future generations.

For my part I, and all my household, were to be circumcised. This was not a condition to receiving His promise, but a permanent reminder to us that He would always be our God. My wife's name was also to be changed: she would become Sarah. She would be blessed and become the mother of nations. I bowed down to the ground when I heard this; mostly because I was in the presence of Almighty God, but also because, I'm afraid, I was trying not to laugh. I was ninety-nine years old, for goodness sake. We hadn't done much in the way of biology when I was at school, but it seemed unlikely that Sarah would now bear children at her age. Yet God repeated His words. He even told me that we were to have a boy and should call him Isaac.

I obeyed, but I think God knew that I wasn't entirely convinced.

And so it happened that I was sitting outside my tent on a particularly hot day when I saw three travellers coming towards me. It is a strict rule of my people that we offer hospitality to all. So I urged them to rest a while and I would provide some food to sustain them as they continued their journey. They agreed, and I hurried inside to tell Sarah that we had guests (You didn't think I was going to make the bread myself, did you?). I told the servant to prepare an animal and I waited on them as they ate. Then one of them said that when He returned this way the following year, Sarah would have a child in her arms. Sarah heard this from inside the tent and then it was her turn to laugh. But God heard her and reminded me that nothing was too difficult for Him.

Sure enough, He kept His word and did for Sarah exactly what He had promised. Months later, she gave birth. We had a son. It was a wonderful, joyous, incredible time. God kept His promise. My estate and wealth would not pass to my slave; we had a son! We named him Isaac, as I had previously been told, which means "laughter." We had both laughed when we had received this promise, so it could have been an embarrassing reminder of the fact. But Sarah pointed out that Isaac would bring us laughter, and that all our friends would laugh, and rejoice, with us.

And it was so. We did have several years of laughter, joy and wonder with this boy; seeing the world through his eyes, revelling in new experiences, and watching God's promise and blessing to us grow before us. We dared to consider the future: our name would continue, and we might yet live to see grandchildren. Almighty God had spoken to me, given His promise and made a covenant with me. I had done nothing to deserve that, and much to thwart it. But He was faithful. We had a son, and I felt twenty years younger.

Then I received the command to kill him.

> *"Take your son, your only son whom you love, Isaac, and sacrifice him as a burnt offering"* (Genesis 22:2).

Wait, what...?

God wanted me to sacrifice my son; the one who had been promised to us, ended our years of shame and brought us so much joy. Was Almighty God angry with me? Was it even God who was speaking? Had I lost it?

I didn't sleep much that night.

What had Isaac, or I, done to deserve this? What about God's promise that I would have many descendants? What about the years of waiting? What about His covenant? Was I going to witness His promise to me literally go up in smoke?

I don't know how I didn't fall to the ground weeping; clinging onto Isaac, begging God to take my own life instead. I don't know why I didn't plead with Him, as I had pleaded with Him to save the unholy city of Sodom. I just know that Isaac, the two servants and I set out the next day, on what would be the longest three days of my life. Not even the wrench of leaving my father's house and my own country without knowing where I was going, had brought as much pain.

I recognised the place as soon as I saw it, and instructed the servants to stay with the donkey, while my son and I went to worship. Worship!

How could I worship, honour and thank Someone who was about to take everything from me, and in the cruellest way imaginable?

But Almighty God, who owed me nothing but had given me so much, had spoken.

I could see that Isaac was puzzled and asked why we had nothing to sacrifice to God. I told him,

"God Himself will provide the lamb for the burnt offering, my son" (Genesis 22:8).

I wasn't sure that I really believed that but I didn't, for one minute, want him to suspect the truth.

I couldn't look him in the eye as I tied him up – why didn't he struggle? – nor as I raised the knife to strike the blow which would end his life, my hopes, my dreams and probably my marriage too. Then God spoke to me again. He told me not to hurt Isaac in any way. He now knew that I was prepared to obey him, even if I didn't understand, even if the command seemed unthinkable. I felt weak with sheer relief and looked to heaven with gratitude. As I did I noticed a ram in a thicket. So I took that and offered it in a sacrifice; one of true worship and thankfulness. Almighty God then repeated His promise that I would have many descendants and that all people would be blessed because of them.

It had been a test.

God wanted to know whether I would give up the most precious thing in my life if He asked me to do so. Was that fair of Him?

Well, He had made me so He had the right to tell me what He wanted from me. He had called me, so He had the right to see if I would faithfully obey and follow. I was willing to obey and trust Him; through tears and gritted teeth, but I was willing. God then gave me back my son and provided a ram to die in his place. I never told Sarah what had nearly happened; it would have been the death of her. As it happened, she did die a short while afterwards, but she never knew the events of that day. A year or so after that, Isaac found a woman; a relative, actually, to marry. This comforted both of us after Sarah's death, though she would have loved an opportunity to buy a new hat. Isaac and Rebekah later gave me twin grandsons. God's promise was unfolding.

And that is my story or, at least, the highlights from it.

I have known great joy and great sorrow in my life. Yet El Shaddai, the One who made me, has been faithful and constantly present.

I hope that my son, who was a great blessing to us and brought laughter and hope, will do the same for others.

GILL TAGGART

AS TOLD BY

Chapter 3
The Scammer
As Told by Jacob

My name is Jacob. My grandfather was Abraham, my father was Isaac and I have a twin brother – Esau. Apparently, I was born holding onto his heel; my name means "he grasps the heel" or "he deceives." I was often in trouble as I lived up to the name that I had been given (Well, what did they expect?). We may have been twins, but Esau and I were quite different. He loved hunting for game and was, I felt, Dad's favourite. He was also smug in the knowledge that, one day, father's blessing would be his; all that wealth and privilege, just because fate allowed him to be born a few minutes before me.

One day, my brother returned from hunting for game. "Quick, give me some of that red stew. I'm famished," he proclaimed, dramatically. I was preparing a meal for the family, so he would have got some eventually. But he thought he could snap his fingers and be given what he wanted when he wanted it. Just because he was the eldest. That gave me an idea. "First sell me your birthright," I told him. I didn't think such a thing was possible – nothing could change the fact that he was the eldest after all. But I was curious to see if his privileged position meant anything to him. Esau agreed. I don't know if he had really thought things through.

Time passed.

Dad was now an old and wealthy man. He couldn't live forever, and then his money would be mine as holder of Esau's birthright. But would it? I had acquired this birthright many years before, there had been no witnesses and I don't think Dad had ever been told. Should I tell my father that the blessing was rightly mine? Would he honour the deal? Would Esau deny it? There was only one thing for it: Dad would have to think that he was blessing his eldest son. After some time, my father did send for Esau and asked him to prepare some game so that he could eat before he gave his blessing. This was my chance. Mum overheard and told me to go to our flock, select two choice goats to make Dad's favourite meal and then take the food to him. I did so. My brother was a hairy man, so I also covered my arms with goats' skins and borrowed some of his clothes. Dad was surprised that "Esau" had returned so quickly from his task, but I told him that God had helped me. Well, it wasn't too far from the truth. I then received the blessing of the firstborn – which was rightfully mine anyway, as Esau himself had decided. Esau was furious when he found out and vowed to kill me after Dad had died. Mum advised me to go and stay with her brother, Laban, in Harran[2] for a while. She managed to arrange it so that Dad thought it had been his idea and I left. I never saw my mother again. That was the price we both paid for that incident.

My journey to Harran required an overnight stop, and

it was then that I had the most amazing dream. In this dream, angels were walking up and down a great stairway, or ladder, which started on Earth and reached up to the heavens. Although I could not see the top of the ladder, I knew God was standing there. It was incredible; I had been given a glimpse of the entrance to heaven. Then God spoke to me. He told me that He was the God of my grandfather and father, who would give me the land on which I was lying and that I would have many descendants and all the nations of the earth would be blessed through me.

I didn't know what to say.

I supposed God would have been angry with me for the way I had treated my brother. Yes, Esau was an annoying little twerp, but he was my twin. I could have tried to get on better with him and been more supportive. Instead, I tricked him and received what was not mine to take (I guess "seeing" God had given me more than a twinge of remorse.). But instead of condemnation or rebuke, this God was going to bless and protect me. That was a truly amazing dream that I'd had and this was an awesome place. God was here! God was here, and I hadn't even been aware of it.

The next morning I took the stone which had been my pillow, set it up as a memorial and poured oil over it. I renamed the place "Bethel" – which means "House of God." I had met God personally, been accepted and blessed by Him and would no longer think of Him as my father's God. Then I moved on.

I eventually arrived at my uncle's home in Harran, planning to stay there for a few weeks. It had to be over twenty years before I left. After I had been working for Laban for about a month, he told me that I shouldn't have to work for free just because we were related and asked me how much I wanted in wages. I had already met my cousin Rachel before I arrived at the house. She was beautiful. Having spent a month now with the family, I was smitten. So I told my uncle that I would gladly work for him for seven years, provided I could marry my youngest cousin. He agreed. I don't know why I settled on the figure of seven years, it sounded like a long time. But in fact, it was over in no time. Seven years, seeing the love of my life every day – no hardship at all.

I was so happy on my wedding day. But, unknown to me, Laban brought Leah, Rachel's plain-looking older sister, to me after dark. When I awoke in the morning, there she was! "What have you done?" I raged at Laban. "I worked seven years for Rachel; why have you tricked me?" Some would have said that the scammer had been scammed. I was beginning to see that it wasn't much fun being on the receiving end. My uncle tried to tell me that it was their custom to marry off the older daughter first, so he'd had no choice. But I wasn't having that. I had asked to marry Rachel and he had agreed. How could he do this to me? But all the raging in the world wasn't going to solve the problem: I was married to Leah and not to Rachel. Laban may have realised that he had gone too far because he said that I could marry Rachel at the end of that week. I had to work for him for another seven years, but at least I would be married to the love of my life. I agreed and after we got married I decided to honour this agreement, even though I was tempted to run off immediately. And so it was that I came to have two wives, but I loved only Rachel.

During our marriage, Leah gave me six sons in total, which she regarded as divine compensation for being unloved and treated as second best. Rachel wasn't able to have children. She became jealous and suggested that I sleep with her slave girl to give her children. This arrangement gave us another two boys. Leah then demanded the same deal which brought our total to ten sons. Finally, my beloved Rachel became pregnant and gave me my eleventh son. We called him Joseph. With two wives, eleven sons and several servants, I thought that it was probably about time that we moved on. Laban's sons were also grumbling and saying that I had acquired my wealth from their father through trickery. I didn't feel that was true, and they could have made trouble for me.

We left. Laban followed in hot pursuit three days later, annoyed that I had gone without telling him. He had not been able to say "goodbye" to his daughters and grandsons. Harsh words followed. Laban accused me of kidnapping his daughters and of deception. I reminded him that, for the most part, I had been his unpaid worker. When he did start paying me, he changed my wages ten times. He had made employment a condition for my marriage, and then he had switched brides on me. But eventually, my uncle suggested that we draw up a covenant between us and our family should be at peace. It left me thinking that it was probably time I did the same with my twin brother, whose crimes had not been nearly so bad. And it was so.

Afterwards, I returned to Bethel and built an altar. There, the Lord appeared to me, revealed His name (El Shaddai) to me and changed mine from Jacob to Israel. We left Bethel and moved onward, towards Bethlehem. With all the drama of the previous few months, I had almost forgotten that my beloved was pregnant again. I remembered when her labour pains began on the road, far from our destination. They were very intense and it was a difficult birth. Tragically, as we welcomed our twelfth boy into the world, my darling wife died. I named my son "Benjamin", buried Rachel, set up a memorial stone and moved on.

I had been greatly blessed with many children, their partners and grandchildren – a large family, as God had promised. We had many blessings, but there were many dramas too. Dinah, my daughter, was shamefully raped one day and her brothers went overboard in their revenge, killing all the inhabitants of the town where the perpetrators had lived. My oldest son, Reuben, slept with my concubine Bilhah, who had been Rachel's handmaid, and was mother to two of my sons. Another of my sons, Judah, had children with his own daughter-in-law. Then there was their behaviour towards Joseph. It's possible that I didn't help matters there. I told myself that I loved my sons equally, but Joseph was the long-awaited son of my beloved wife. Whereas, to my shame, I hadn't loved Leah – the mother to some of my other boys. Maybe I spoilt Joseph for that very reason. Maybe he played on it and was precocious, especially after receiving dreams which had seemed to speak of power and leadership. Perhaps he was boasting when he recounted them to the rest of the family, or perhaps he was insecure, wanting reassurance that it was God who had spoken to him. But did he deserve to be attacked by his brothers, flung into a pit and then sold into slavery? I am told it was Judah who suggested this latter course of action, which almost certainly saved his life. The others had intended to kill him.

Should they have led me to think he was dead, though? Did I deserve that? Didn't they care about my grief and what that news might have done to me? That part of our story had a happy ending – better, in fact, than I could have ever imagined. There was a famine in our land and the lads – minus Benjamin, the only remaining child of my beloved – had to go to Egypt to buy food. There they met with Pharaoh's second-in-command who heard their story, seemed to take a curious interest in them and demanded that Benjamin be brought to him. He said he would not believe that they were honest men otherwise. He had them locked up for spying. They might have remained there, as I was adamant that I was not going to lose Rachel's second child. But Judah pointed out that we would not get food if Benjamin were not with us and guaranteed his safety. I understand that Ben then nearly got locked up in

Egypt due to some misunderstanding, but that Judah begged for his release and even offered to take his place in jail. Was it guilt over Joseph, or remorse over his own behaviour towards his daughter-in-law which prompted this sacrificial offer? I'll never know. But it wasn't important. Pharaoh's second-in-command turned out to be my Joseph. He had been as good as dead and now he was alive. That was a happy reunion.

And that is my story: one of deceit, love, struggle, pain, loss, tears and great joy. I was once Jacob, the "deceiver." I deceived, had been deceived and have deserved none of the blessings which I received. But Almighty God, who sees all, cannot be deceived. He renamed me "Israel", has also blessed me, kept His promise and has never left me. I will soon bless my sons, for my time here is short. Reuben, my eldest, deserves no blessing; he has sullied my name. Simeon and Levi exacted a terrible revenge for their sister's treatment. Their loyalty was commendable but I fear, and cannot condone, their anger. Joseph, son of my beloved, had been dead, then he was alive again. He is a fruitful vine and will be greatly blessed by God. The name Judah means "praise" and he, mostly, has a good heart. He protected Benjamin and guaranteed his safety, at the cost of his sons. It will be through Judah's descendants that the Chosen One will come.

> *"The sceptre will not depart from Judah, nor the ruler's staff from between his feet, until he to whom it belongs shall come"* (Genesis 49:10).

I don't know where those words came from, but that is my blessing for Judah. My sons are the heads of twelve families, or tribes. They are blessed and are all loved by God. Yet the tribe of Judah will be chosen through which to fulfil God's coming purposes.

I wonder what those purposes might be.

GILL TAGGART

AS TOLD BY

Chapter 4
Arguing with God
As Told by Moses

My name is Moses. My father was called "Amram", my mother was "Jochebed" (Exodus 6:20) and my great, great grandfather was Jacob. I am a Hebrew brought up in Egypt. I was born at a difficult time for my people. Years before, Jacob and his family had come to Egypt to escape a famine. They settled there and grew greatly in number, which alarmed Pharaoh who thought that they might form an army and fight against him. He reacted towards this by forcing the Hebrews into slave labour. When he failed to crush their spirits through cruelty, he ordered the midwives to kill any male babies that they delivered. The midwives wouldn't, so Pharaoh ordered all male babies to be thrown into the Nile.

It was at this point that I was born. My mother was frightened when she saw that she had given birth to a boy. She seemed to sense, or believe, that I was a special baby (Though I imagine all mothers feel that way about their offspring.). Mother hid me for three months and then decided to outwit Pharaoh. If Pharaoh wanted me in the Nile, she would put me in the Nile: in a watertight wicker basket.

And it was so. My basket was soon noticed as it drifted down the river. I could have ended up anywhere but, as it happened, Pharaoh's daughter was bathing at the water's edge and heard me crying. I think she might have taken me there and then, but my sister, who had been keeping watch, asked if she should go and find someone to nurse me for a few months. Pharaoh's daughter thought that a good idea, so I, temporarily, ended up back at home. How amazing that my mother, who had placed me in the river to save my life, not knowing if she would ever see me again, should be paid to become my nurse. How amazing that I should be rescued by the daughter of the one who had given orders to kill me, and, later, brought up in his palace right under his nose. I was given the name Moses because I had been "drawn out of the water". Of course, this didn't "just happen", nor was it just "amazing", but rather the plan of the One who made me.

So I grew up in luxury. The son of a despised Hebrew slave, a child whom Pharaoh had tried to kill, was now his adopted grandson. I think I always knew of my adoption and my roots, but I felt it keenly one day when I saw an Egyptian fighting with a Hebrew slave. So indignant was I that I killed the Egyptian. Then I buried him and ran off. The next day I saw two more men fighting. These were both Hebrews – which puzzled me. They should have been saving their ire for their oppressors, not each other. Imagine my shock when it became clear that one of these men had seen me kill the Egyptian the previous day. What had I done? Never mind my lofty connections, I had killed an Egyptian. Word would get around and Pharaoh would kill me.

This time, I ran and didn't return. I fled to Midian and,

after helping some women who were being threatened over their rights to water, found myself in the tent of Jethro – their father. Jethro and his family were very welcoming. I stayed with them and later married the eldest daughter, Zipporah. Back in Egypt, Pharaoh had died, yet someone equally as ruthless had taken his place. The Hebrew slaves who were, after all, my people, were desperate; trapped in slavery under a cruel and harsh regime.

Unknown to me, they were crying out to God for help.

Unknown to me, God was about to answer them.

One day, I was out tending to the sheep. There was nothing unusual in that – I had been doing it for years. Each day brought new challenges: Would one of the animals get injured, give birth, die or need to be rescued from a wolf? Most of the time, things were fairly predictable though – nothing much out of the ordinary happened. Not this day.

We came to Mount Horeb, which some have called "the Mountain of God", and there was a bush that was on fire. There was nothing very extraordinary about that. It often happens in this dry climate. I went over to take a closer look but, strangely, the bush wasn't burnt. There seemed to be flames coming from it, yet it wasn't even singed. And then I heard Someone calling my name. The Voice told me not to go any closer and to take off my shoes as I was standing on holy ground. He said that He, the God of Abraham, Isaac and Jacob, had seen the suffering of the Hebrew slaves and was going to act. God was going to save them from slavery.

Astonishing.

For some reason, it astonished me more that He told me about it first than that He was going to intervene.

"I'm sorry, what? You want me to go to Pharaoh and tell him to let the Hebrew slaves, his workforce, leave Egypt? Errr, I don't think You quite understand the situation, God. No one challenges Pharaoh – ever. Not if they value their lives, anyway." He was regarded as a god. I would be going to the most powerful man in the land with a request – no, an order – from the Lord.

My God would be challenging this god. If I was to do something as difficult as this, I needed to be certain that it really was God speaking to me – and I didn't even know His name.

So He told me.

Abraham, Isaac and Jacob had known Him as "El Shaddai", the all-powerful, almighty One. He was still that. But now He revealed Himself to me as "I AM WHO I AM". I was to go to my people and tell them that "I AM" had sent me to them and that He promised "to bring you up out of your misery in Egypt" (Exodus 3:17). The God of the Israelites – of Abraham, Isaac and Jacob – had revealed Himself to me too; I truly was one of His people! I wasn't happy with my task, however. I was eighty years old, for goodness sake. There was no reason for anyone, least of all Pharaoh, to listen to me and I couldn't speak very well. All good reasons, I thought, why I shouldn't do this. But God wasn't listening, He answered all my objections and said that He would be with me – not to mention my brother, Aaron. He became rather angry at my continued excuses, so I gave in. I soon found out, however, that Pharaoh had no intention of giving in. The Egyptians suffered plague after plague because Pharaoh was not willing to listen to the Hebrew God.

I wish he had listened.

I wish he'd heeded the first few plagues; then, he could have spared the Egyptians further suffering. Had he not repeatedly gone back on his word and tried to defy God, there would not have been that final plague – the death of the firstborn son, which killed his own son. We were told to leave soon afterwards. It sounds easy when you say it like that, but try getting around a million families, children and all their belongings out of a country! The older family members couldn't walk quickly, if at all. Young men were keen to get going. Young mothers were trying to organise their noisy, excited, frightened children. Some people were sick, dying and needed care; some women were pregnant or in labour. Then there were the animals. I had several willing helpers, but it still took a lot of organisation.

At first, our journey was straightforward: People were happy, excited, hopeful and full of praise to the God who had rescued them. It's easy to trust when life is good. But it wasn't long before there were problems.

We weren't led out along the main road – that would have meant going through enemy territory and I think God knew that if we were faced with a battle so early on, the people would panic. So we journeyed through the wilderness to the Red Sea. Back in Egypt Pharaoh, having learnt nothing from the plagues, was rallying his soldiers and preparing to give chase. So there we were with the Red Sea ahead of us; Pharaoh's soldiers behind us (and a few hundred thousand disgruntled people blaming me and demanding to know why I had not left them in Egypt).

I was so disappointed with them. All the displays of God's power had been shown: the Nile turning to blood, the frog, flies, hail and various other plagues which showed that our God had control over the elements. Yet faced with a problem or challenge, the nation's reaction was to complain. I was told to pick up my staff and raise it over the sea. The people were told to keep moving forward to the water's edge; which most did, after some more prolonged grumbling. There was a strong wind so powerful that even the most sure-footed were almost knocked off balance. The grumbling turned to gasps and I think some screamed. But before us, slowly but surely, the waters of the sea began to part until finally, there was a defined path through the middle. By this time, the soldiers were almost at the water's edge (or at least, where the water's edge had once been). The people stopped grumbling and screaming and began to cross as quickly as they could. Then, when all were safely on the other side, I lowered my staff with a sense of relief. My arms were going numb. The waters of the Red Sea began to flow back over the soldiers, horsemen and chariots which had begun to cross.

We were safe. I didn't know what Pharaoh would make of it all or whether he would finally come to believe in God. That wasn't my concern. However, compared with what I faced in that wilderness, I sometimes think that dealing with Pharaoh would have been the easier option. Besides all the miracles in Egypt, the Hebrew slaves could now testify that God had parted the sea itself to keep them safe. Sadly this wasn't enough to cause them to trust in God's care and protection.

We came to Marah, where we found that the water was too bitter to drink. The people grumbled, God fixed it and the people rejoiced. The people complained that they didn't have enough food: God gave us a substance called "manna" and the people rejoiced. The people complained that they were sick of eating nothing but manna: God provided quail and the people rejoiced. We ran out of water again. The people grumbled. God provided and the people rejoiced. Every trial was an opportunity to look back and remember how God had previously provided. Yet every trial led to the complaint that the nation would have been better off staying in Egypt. I should say that not everyone behaved like this. A few men were loyal, and there was one other notable exception – my father-in-law. When Jethro heard how God had rescued the nation from Egypt and miraculously provided, he became a believer. He also became my fervent supporter and gave me the valuable advice of not trying to manage everyone's problems on my own, but to appoint seventy leaders to help shoulder the burdens and complaints that came my way (there were many of those). We came to Mount Sinai where God would give us His Word and make a covenant with us. Following God's instructions, the people stayed at the base of the mountain, purified themselves and waited. They seemed keen for me to speak to God for them – possibly afraid to receive from the God they had grumbled against. So I went alone to speak face to face with the God who called Himself "I AM." I received His instructions, His law and His covenant that was to be made between Him and His people.

That is my story. Who would have thought that Almighty God would choose a disorganised, disobedient group of slaves to become His people and to be an example to others? Who would have thought that an eighty-year-old fugitive, wanted for murder, would get to speak to this God face to face? None of those who left Egypt as slaves will get to enter the Promised Land, apart from Joshua and Caleb, who were prepared to trust God when all others trusted only the evidence of their eyes. The name Joshua means "he saves." He will teach the nation to trust in the God who saved them from slavery and made them His people. He has shown faith and trust in the God who saved us – a leader needs those qualities if he is to inspire them in others. I have seen the Promised Land, but I am not to enter it. I will soon rest with our fathers.

I wonder what will become of God's people.

AS TOLD BY

Chapter 5
The Widows
As Told by Naomi and Ruth

Naomi

My name is Naomi and my husband's name was Elimelech. We lived in Bethlehem, in Judah, but moved to Moab after a severe famine hit the land. It's a shame that the Moabites and Israelites haven't always got on well, as the father of the nation of Moab, was Abraham's great-nephew. I feel the Israelites have sometimes thought themselves superior because God made a covenant with and blessed Abraham and not his brother. But the people of Moab were good to us when we arrived there as refugees.

Sadly my husband died soon after this. I blamed it on the stress of the move. We grieved. After a while, we began to settle in our new land and my sons, Kilion and Mahlon, married Moabite women – Orpah and Ruth. Neither couple had children, but for the next ten years, life was good. Then, tragically, my sons died too.

I was desolate.

All three of them were taken within a few years. Why was this happening to me? Why would God allow it to happen to me? I didn't even have the comfort of grandchildren. I had no one, except for my two daughters-in-law.

In time I heard that the Lord had been good to my homeland (Why hadn't He been good to me?) and provided them with many crops. So I decided to return. There was nothing here for me anymore. We set off for Bethlehem. But after a while, I began to wonder if I should be taking Orpah and Ruth away from their family. I had nothing to offer them and they might as well return to their homeland. Orpah needed a little persuading but eventually did so. Ruth, however, refused and told me, "Your people will be my people and your God, my God" (Ruth 1:16). I don't know why she wanted to stay with me. I had nothing. But I was touched by her loyalty and love. When we reached Bethlehem, the women seemed pleased to see me. "Could this be Naomi?" they exclaimed. But I was sad and angry. "Don't call me Naomi," (which means 'pleasant') I told them, "Call me Mara." It means, "bitter." "Because the Almighty has made my life very bitter" (Ruth 1:19–20).

It was the start of the barley harvest – a busy time. One day, Ruth asked me if she could go into the fields to pick up the ears of wheat which were dropped by the men who were harvesting. It was a daring thing to suggest, but we had to eat, so I agreed.

I was astonished when she returned that evening and told me that she had been gathering in the field of a man named Boaz. "That man is one of our closest relatives, one of our family redeemers," I told her. I was delighted when Ruth said that Boaz wanted her to return to the field the next day, and from then on until the harvest had been gathered. Of all the fields that Ruth could have picked! Or could it be a sign that God was with us, and looking out for us, after all?

Ruth continued to work in the fields and, for a while, life was good. But, even though she hadn't so much as hinted about a future, I couldn't help feeling that I should try to find a home and a husband for her. Oh, no one could replace my Mahlon, but Ruth was still a young, attractive woman. And who better to be her husband than Boaz? He was related to my late husband, so he had a duty to care for us and had already shown himself to be kind and trustworthy. I told Ruth of my thoughts and instructed her to bathe, put on her finest clothes and then go to the threshing floor that evening. But she was not to let Boaz see her. She was to watch where he lay down, then remove his cloak and lay down at his feet. She would, effectively, be saying to him, "I place myself under your protection. Please take care of me." Men are sometimes slow to take a hint or to act, but even he could not have missed the clear meaning of her actions.

And it was so. Boaz seemed to recognise that, by not looking for a husband of her own age, her main concern was for me, and was touched by Ruth's loyalty. I was told that he addressed her as "daughter," which was an indication of acceptance into the family, rather than a dig about the age gap. Ruth left the threshing floor early the next morning, without being seen. I was delighted when I heard that my daughter-in-law had not been rejected, but not so pleased when I heard that there was a closer kinsman-redeemer than Boaz. I knew nothing about him. I didn't want that. I wanted Ruth to marry Boaz. Yet I also felt that I could trust Boaz, and maybe God, to sort everything out. I later heard that this other relative had been eager to buy my late husband's land but didn't realise that this meant that Ruth and I were part of the deal. This man would have to marry Ruth himself, provide her with children and keep the land, and her husband's name, in the family. Thankfully for us, he was not prepared to do this. Boaz married Ruth and, in time, had a son.

That is my story. I lost everything and suffered sorrow and pain. But God was with me, even in the dark times, and now I have a family again.

I hope that they, and others, will know and follow the God who saves and blesses.

Ruth

My name is Ruth. I am from Moab, but I was married to a man from Bethlehem after the family came to settle in my country. Sadly, my father-in-law died a while later. But I still had my husband, Mahlon, his brother Kilion and his wife, Orpah. About ten years later, however, my husband and brother-in-law died too. I heard whispers that this was a judgement because they had left Israel and their god, had settled in a foreign land and married non-Israelite women – which their god did not allow. I'm not sure if

I believe that.

My mother-in-law, Naomi, was understandably distraught at losing the men in her life. There were no grandchildren to comfort her, so we set off to return to Bethlehem, where the family had lived. On the way, Naomi seemed keen for us to return to our own country and our former lives. Orpah eventually, but I think reluctantly, agreed. But I had grown fond of Naomi and wanted to see where my husband had grown up. So I insisted and told her that, from now on, her people would be my people; her God, my God. I didn't feel that was a particularly heroic thing to say. There was little for me in my country. Everyone knew that I had married an Israelite and I had nothing to lose. It also comforted me to give Mahlon's mother a little comfort.

We found somewhere to stay and I tried to adjust to my new life. One day I suggested to Naomi that I might go into the fields and pick up any ears of corn that the reapers had left behind. I was told that poor people were allowed to do that, and we might get a few loaves of bread from what I gathered. I found myself in the field of a wealthy man called Boaz who, unknown to me, was a relative of my late father-in-law. He noticed me and asked whom I belonged to. He was told that I had come from Moab with Naomi and that I was a hard worker. He came over to me. Had I done wrong by working in his field, I wondered. But no, he spoke kindly to me and suggested that I walk behind the other women, rather than work on my own. Boaz also said that I could help myself to water that the men had drawn from the well. I was surprised that the owner was willing to talk to a foreign woman. But he replied that he knew who I was and of the kindness I had shown to Naomi after she was widowed. I could have said that I was widowed too and that it was no hardship to look after my mother-in-law. But I thought I had better keep silent, and simply thanked him for his care. He was a generous man. He allowed me to sit with him when it was time for the meal; I had never before had so much to eat. And when I went back to work, not only did he tell his men not to cause me any trouble, but he also even instructed them to drop some of their wheat, on purpose, so that I could pick it up. Such kindness.

Naomi could hardly believe it when I returned that evening with a huge basket of wheat and she then asked me how I had found so much. I told her that the man who had helped me was called Boaz. She was overjoyed: "That man is one of our closest relatives!" I said that this man had also told me to go back and stay with his harvesters until the harvest was over, which I did. Truly someone, maybe even Naomi's God, was looking after us.

I continued to work in the fields and live with Naomi and found life to be pleasant. But one day, Naomi said that she needed to find a permanent home, and, the implication was, another husband for me. I had accepted Naomi's people and God but I was still, essentially, a single woman and a foreigner. Naomi seemed to have Boaz himself in mind as a husband for me. He had been so kind, and he was a family relative. It seemed that he had a duty to care for us.

So Naomi instructed me to put on my nicest clothes, wear some perfume and go to the threshing floor, but not to let Boaz see me until he had finished eating and drinking. Then, I was to notice where he lay down, uncover his feet and lay down beside him. I still did not fully know the ways of these people – was it normal for a woman to approach a man in this way? Not only was I asking to share his cloak, but I was asking for his protection and care. I did not know what his reaction would be, but I trusted Naomi who was, after all, older than I. So that's what I did. Boaz woke in the night and found a woman at his feet and a proposition of marriage. Amazingly, and thankfully, he was not annoyed, nor put off by my words. He seemed pleased that I had not gone after a younger man. He assured me that he would do what was necessary. However, he then stated that, though we were fairly closely related, there was someone in the town who was an even closer relative. The convention stated that this man should be the one to marry me. I lay down beside him that night feeling confused. Boaz, in whose field I had "happened" to arrive, who had shown me such kindness, generosity and care, was now saying that I might have to marry a stranger. I left early the next morning, without his promise to care for me, but with enough grain to feed Naomi and me for several days.

True to his word, Boaz wasted no time in taking action. He went to the town gate, where townsmen and foreigners met to talk business, or sort out legal matters, and sat down. It wasn't too long before the closer relative came by. My late father-in-law had owned a small piece of land which he had leased, during the famine, to someone from outside the family. This land could not be sold. It had to remain in the family and be "redeemed" by someone in the clan. Boaz said that this man was entitled to buy this land since he was Naomi's closer relative. The man agreed that he would redeem it on behalf of Naomi. To do that, the man needed to take off his sandal and give it to Boaz in the presence of ten witnesses. All legal business was conducted at the town gate, so the latter would not have been a problem. Naomi and I were going to belong to a stranger!

Boaz then pointed out that the man would have to redeem it on my behalf, also. This was more difficult, as the man would then be obliged to marry me. If we had children, our son would be named as heir of the land. As this kinsman-redeemer already had a family, he felt unable to do this and said that Boaz could redeem us if he so wished.

And it was so. It was not only the ten required men who were witnesses to this, but all the people of the town had gathered at the gate to see, and approve, this transaction. I had been redeemed. I was able to marry Boaz and our family's reputation would be restored. More than that, I was no longer an outsider – a foreign woman. I had been welcomed and accepted by Naomi's people and God; who were now my people and my God. I belonged. These dear people blessed Boaz, in the name of our God and asked that the Lord might make me like Rachael and Leah: two very important, and fertile, women, from whom the twelve tribes of Israel had come. It was an amazing wedding. This new, adopted family of mine knew how to celebrate! The festivities went on for several days. And then, it seemed like only five minutes later, we welcomed our little boy into the world. Oh, he had no idea how loved, special and important he was. He was the child of our union, a blessing from our God. He was also our redeemer; someone to bear Mahlon's name.

That is my story. I was a foreigner, an outsider who didn't know God. Yet He cared for me, redeemed me and placed me into a family.

I wonder if others have been outsiders and know that God can care for them too.

AS TOLD BY

Chapter 6
The Adulterous King
As Told by David

My name is David. My father is called Jesse and my great grandfather was Boaz, who was married to Ruth. My ninth great grandfather was Jacob. We are from the tribe of Judah and live in Bethlehem. I am the youngest son and I look after our sheep.

One day, one of my brothers came and ushered me in from the field. When I reached the house I saw Dad, my brothers and the prophet Samuel waiting. I wondered what had happened. But then, to my surprise, the prophet Samuel came over to me and anointed me in front of everyone. I didn't know what to think. People are usually only anointed as prophets or kings. We already had a king, and I wasn't a prophet. Nor did I really want to be. I was just looking after sheep. Things did change somewhat after that. I was summoned to court one day. They wanted a musician for King Saul. It seems the poor man was troubled and depressed and music helped to soothe him.

During those years, the Philistines were still making their presence felt. One day their champion, Goliath – who was nine feet tall, heavily built and heavily armed – came into the camp and started to mock Israel and our God,

AS TOLD BY

"This day I defy the armies of Israel! Give me a man and let us fight each other" (1 Samuel 17:10).

Needless to say, no one wanted to take up the challenge. This carried on every day, for about forty days and became humiliating (as well as rather tedious). One day, Dad asked me to go down to the battle lines, where my brothers were, to make sure that they were well. I arrived just as Goliath was making his usual threat. I also heard someone saying that the king was offering a reward: wealth and his daughter's hand in marriage and exemption from taxes. Well, I wasn't too concerned about wealth and hadn't thought much about marriage, but our family would benefit from not having to pay taxes. Besides, this pagan was mocking the God who made me, and whom I loved, and I felt that something had to be done. My oldest brother, Eliab, heard me speaking to the men and became quite angry. He seemed to think I was only good for tending sheep, but I had a right to at least find out what was going on. I asked to see King Saul and offered to go and take on this "champion." King Saul was astounded and reminded me that Goliath had been a warrior since he was my age. But I was used to protecting sheep from wild animals. Only recently, I had had to rescue a terrified ewe from the jaws of a lion, just before it had tried to kill her. God had been with me then and was with me now.

I don't know if anyone was convinced or if they were just desperate, but they handed me a coat of mail and a bronze helmet to put on. "I can't go in these," I protested, "I'm not used to them." I could barely move. So I went out to face him without them: just me, my catapult and five stones from a nearby stream. Goliath was both amused and scornful when he saw the man that Israel had put forward to fight him, and he cursed me in the name of his gods. But I stood firm (partly to stop my knees from shaking) and answered that I came to him in the name of my God, the Lord Almighty (El Shaddai). "This very day," I said, "the Lord will deliver you into my hands. Then the whole world will know that there is a God."

And it was so. The Philistine army turned and ran when they saw that their champion was dead. The Israeli army was rejuvenated, ran after them and defeated them. From then on, I lived in King Saul's palace. I married his daughter and met his son, Jonathan, who became like a brother to me.

I would like to say that we all lived happily ever after, but Saul was an unstable man and jealous of my popularity. I don't know why. I meant him no harm. There were a couple of occasions, while he was chasing me when I could have killed him in his sleep. I didn't. I just took a couple of souvenirs to show him that his life had been in my hands. On each occasion, Saul seemed to realise that, though he had done me wrong, I had repaid him with kindness. But it never lasted for long. His daughter (my wife) and his son Jonathan warned me often of their father's intentions. They saved my life. By this time, I was tired, angry and confused.

Why did Saul wish me harm when I had only ever tried to help him? Why did he want to kill the father of his grandchildren? Why hadn't Samuel waited until Saul was dead before anointing me? But I had to hold onto the belief that the Lord was my shepherd and would lead me to green pastures and still waters. Without that, I had nothing. Saul had once been anointed as king too. Had he forgotten? Had he lost God, or lost sight of the task he had been given to do? I hoped not. Much as I hated what Saul was doing to me, I couldn't help feeling sorry for him.

Then on one dreadful day, I received news that Saul and Jonathan had been killed in battle. I was heartbroken. I can't say that Saul's death didn't give me some feeling of relief and sadness too for what might have been. But Jonathan? He had been like a brother to me and he had, more than once, risked his life for me by standing up to his father. I decided that, although I could do nothing more now for him, I could help any of his living relatives. They told me about Mephibosheth, a man crippled in both legs, so I brought him to court to live with me. People have marvelled at how an unemployed cripple could come to live with a king. Some seem to think that I was either reckless or some sort of saint to do this. But God appointed me to be king when I was a young, unknown shepherd boy, and Saul, for all his faults, took me into his palace. Should I not do the same for the relative of a dear friend?

In the meantime, I was crowned king. The first thing that I did was to bring the Ark of the Covenant, which contained the commandments given to Moses, to Jerusalem. God's name and His presence with us were represented by that Ark, and I meant to show the people that God, our Shepherd and true King, should come first. I wasn't happy that I only had a tent in which to place this Ark. I, a man, was living in comfort and splendour, yet the God who had made me, and the whole universe, deserved so much more. But God spoke to Nathan, the prophet, one night and told him that I was not to build Him a fixed dwelling. He also told Nathan to say,

"Your house and your kingdom shall endure forever before Me; your throne shall be established forever" (2 Samuel 7:16).

I felt overwhelmed when I heard this. Who was I, that Almighty God, El Shaddai, should notice me and bless me so greatly? I asked God to bless me as He had promised and I promised to serve him forever.

How quickly things change.

I would not have believed that, one day soon, I would sin against the God who had called, anointed, strengthened, blessed and encouraged me. I would not have said that I, who loved God's commands, would break them so spectacularly. But that, I'm ashamed to say, is what happened. Maybe I let my guard down. Maybe I had become so complacent, so blessed and favoured by God, that I thought I was untouchable. One spring evening, I was unable to sleep and found myself walking around on the rooftop of my house. As I did, I caught sight of a beautiful woman who was bathing. I had to find out more about her and later learnt that she was Bathsheba, the wife of Uriah. I sent some messengers to bring her to me. I told myself that I wanted to talk to her and maybe offer her a role at my court. I ended up sleeping with her. I knew I had done wrong, but no one else knew, and it was likely that they never would.

That might well have been so, had Bathsheba not become pregnant.

Our law says that a woman is unclean during her monthly period. So afterwards, she must bathe and purify herself. This is what Bathsheba had been doing when I saw her, so I knew the child had to be mine. No one else did, though. So I sent for Uriah, who was fighting for the country and tried to persuade him to go home and seduce his wife. Then, when the child was born, she could say it was his. I should have known that Uriah was a man of principle. He refused to go home, eat, drink and seduce his wife while his men were away fighting. He wouldn't return home, either, after we had dined together and I had got him drunk. This was all going wrong. Folk would soon know that Bathsheba was pregnant and I needed them to believe that the child was her husband's. Maybe if Uriah died in battle, they would refrain from asking awkward questions during Bathsheba's time of mourning.

I asked Joab to post Uriah onto the front line and was secretly relieved when I later heard that he had been killed. What a mess we sometimes get into when we disobey God. How much worse we make it for ourselves when we can't even admit our mistakes, or deliberate acts, but try instead to cover them up? Do we really think we can fool Almighty God? I had a visit from Nathan, the prophet, who wanted to tell me a story of injustice. It seemed two men were living in a town. One was very rich with many sheep and cattle and the other was very poor and had just one lamb. One day, the rich man had a guest, who needed to offer him a meal but was reluctant to kill any of his own sheep. So he took the one lamb that belonged to the poor man and they ate it. I was furious when I heard this. The man needed to repay the poor man four times over, I declared. He deserved to die. I would not have greed and injustice in my kingdom.

How great was my indignation. How great was my shame when Nathan replied, "You are that man!" He reminded me that God had anointed me as king over Israel, saved me from Saul and given me his palace, his daughter, many riches and more. Why had I despised the Lord and taken the one thing that did not belong to me: another man's wife? I was mortified. There was nothing I could say except, "I have sinned against God." Astonishingly, Nathan said that God had forgiven me. I wouldn't die for my sin. But my newborn child would. I had disobeyed and despised God's Word. My life would be saved; my child's wouldn't. I ate no food and lay on the ground, weeping, praying and pleading with God. Did God forgive me or could He only forgive by removing the evidence of my sin? Was my child taking the punishment that had been meant for me?

They were afraid to tell me when he died.

I had eaten no food while pleading for his life. What then would happen when I knew that it had been in vain? But I surprised myself, and those around me, by bathing, dressing and going to the temple to worship God. Then I returned to the palace for a meal. Why had I done that, they wondered. Why wasn't I weeping and grieving? Didn't I care? Yes, of course, I cared. But I couldn't change what had happened. I had hoped that, if I repented and showed true remorse, there would have been no consequences for me. That wasn't to be. We would not live happily with a constant reminder of our sin. God had taken our child to be with Him. He was safe and one day, I would see him again. I knew also that I should not despise God's Word or hold it lightly. He was the One who had made me, and also our child. He would do what was right and just.

That is not the end of my story. Bathsheba and I had another son, Solomon. One day he will succeed me as king. I have had many joys and sorrows, ups and downs, both with my large family and the nation. I still got things wrong and sometimes sinned. But though I sometimes messed up, I never lost faith in God. Though I knew the misery of sin and punishment, I also knew that God was merciful and forgiving. He was also faithful. He had made an everlasting covenant with me and given a promise that one of my descendants would always be on the throne. God had been with me throughout my life; caring for me, re-directing me if I went astray, bringing me back to green pastures.

I hope that Solomon will also know the God who loves and cares for him.

AS TOLD BY

Chapter 7
The Fire Starter
As Told by Elijah

My name is Elijah and I am a prophet of God. My early life doesn't matter. It was uneventful, even unremarkable, except that my parents gave me my name, which means, "The Lord is God." I was too young to know it, but that was an act of bravery in a nation whose people had forgotten their covenant with God and were worshipping almost anything that moved (and some things that didn't).

My work began in Israel, where Ahab was king. God, the One who made us, had told us that it would not be good to marry women from other countries. It wasn't because there was anything wrong with them, I hasten to add. However, there was a fear that these women would bring their own gods to our country when they got married and that it might turn God's people away from Him and our faith.

And it was so. It was especially so in the case of Ahab, who married Jezebel. While she was queen of my country, she wanted us all to worship her god, "Baal", as she did. We believe there is only one God who is the God of our fathers, Abraham, Isaac and Jacob. We believe that He made and takes care of the world. Other nations believe that there is a god for everything. Baal was the god of fertility; the growth of people, crops, and animals. And he controlled the weather. One of my early assignments was to tell the king, who now worshipped the god who controlled the weather, that there would be no rain in the land until I, the prophet of the Lord, said so. To say that I was nervous would be an understatement. Ahab could have had me killed. But then, had he done so, I would not have been around to restore the rain. Also, I had a sneaking suspicion that he was rather scared of his wife, and more inclined to listen to God than he made out. So I went to him, said my piece, and there was a drought in the land for three years.

During this time, I was sent to hide in the Kerith ravine. I was able to drink from a brook and, surprising as it may sound, ravens brought me food. But the drought was severe and, in time, this brook dried up. I didn't know what to do. I was thirsty, and there was no water. I could understand God wanting to show that He, and not Baal, controlled the weather. But couldn't He have provided for those who didn't worship Baal? I should have realised that He was looking after me. He spoke to me again and told me to go and live with a widow in Zarephath, who had been told to take care of me. I went and saw a woman by the town gate who was gathering sticks. I didn't know whether or not she was "the one", but I was very thirsty by this time, so I asked for a little water. Even though we were in the middle of a drought, and she had no idea who I was, she indicated that she would do this, and went off to fill her jug. As she passed me I called out, "And bring me, please, a piece of bread." She looked so sad. "As surely as the Lord your God lives," she replied, "I don't have any bread." I didn't have time to wonder why God might have sent me to someone who couldn't feed me, because she continued,

"I am gathering a few sticks to take home and make a meal for myself and my son, that we may eat it – and die" (1 Kings 17:12).

I told her not to be afraid. I told her to go home and to make the bread as she had planned, but to bring me a piece first. I assured her that God had spoken to me and told me that she would not run out of flour, or oil, until the drought was over. And this woman, who didn't know me, and had little reason to trust me, did as she was asked. Maybe she thought that it made no difference, since she, and her son, were going to die anyway. I don't know. I just know that it was as I had said. We had many meals together; she did not run out of flour or oil.

After a while, however, the woman's son became ill. Sadly, he got worse and died. His mother, as you can imagine, was distraught. She and her son had been saved from death and miraculously provided for, and then this happened. I didn't understand it either, but I knew that God was not punishing her for her sins, as she supposed. "Give me your son," I said. I took the dead boy, laid him on the bed and prayed. Well actually, I first asked God why He had allowed such a thing to happen after the woman had shown me such kindness. It was madness to talk like this, but God didn't seem to mind my saying what was in my heart. After I prayed, the boy's life returned.

A year or so later, when the drought was in its third year, God spoke to me again. He told me to go to King Ahab and tell him that there would soon be rain. When Ahab saw me, he said, "Is it really you, you troublemaker of Israel?" I ignored and rejected his opinion of me as I had brought no trouble to Israel. "You and your family are the troublemakers," I told him, "For you have refused to obey God's commands." Then I asked him to gather the whole of Israel – along with the prophets of Baal – together and to meet me at Mount Carmel.

"How long will you waver between two opinions?" I asked them. "If the Lord is God, follow Him, but if Baal is god, follow him." I proposed a test. We would sacrifice two bulls and whoever answered by sending fire to burn up the sacrifice, he was God. I was challenging their gods – just as Moses had done with Pharaoh and David had done with Goliath. Yahweh would win, of course, but I needed the people to see, remember and believe. The people agreed. The prophets of Baal went first and called upon their god to answer them. They called, they shouted, they pleaded and then danced for hours around the altar that they had built. Maybe it was unkind, but I couldn't resist a little fun at their expense: "Shout louder! Perhaps he is deep in thought or busy. Maybe he is sleeping and must be awakened" (1 Kings 18:27). The prophets started yelling for all they were worth and even began cutting themselves with knives as was their custom. Nothing.

They waited to see what I would do next. "Fill four

large jars with water," I told them after the shrieking and cavorting had finally come to an end. "Tip them over the sacrifice." I was surprised that anyone obeyed that instruction. We were in a drought, the river was some distance away and the jars were heavy, even when empty. "Now do it twice more," I told them. At the time that we would normally have made the evening sacrifice, I prayed:

> *"God of Abraham, Isaac and Israel, let it be known today that you are God in Israel... Answer me, Lord, so that these people will know that you are turning their hearts back again"* (1 Kings 18:37).

Fire blazed from heaven. It was so hot, that it even dried up the water that had filled the trench. The people fell to their knees and cried out, "The Lord – He is God!"

A great victory, you might think. The people had seen the Lord's power. Surely their hearts would be changed and they would, again, worship the one, true God. I couldn't celebrate though. I had seen this kind of fickle behaviour before. The crowd proclaimed God in the joy of victory. But what if things went wrong again and something else began to look more enticing? I felt I needed to make my point; so I ordered the people to seize all four hundred and fifty prophets of Baal, and we put them to death. Then I told Ahab that he needed to prepare for a rainstorm. While he was pondering this, I climbed up Mount Carmel and prayed. Seven times I instructed my servant to go and look out to sea; six times he returned saying he could see nothing. But upon the seventh time, he told me that he could see a small cloud about the size of a man's hand. We just got to Jezreel before the rain started.

I was exhausted. I wasn't completely sure if killing all the prophets of Baal had been a good idea after all. Had God told me to do it or had I just decided to show them that I meant business? Was it an act of zeal or anger? I didn't know. But Jezebel did and, in her fury, vowed to do the same to me. I ran to Beersheba, in Judah, and from there, into the wilderness. "Lord, I've had enough," I said. Jezebel wanted me dead anyway, so I thought that the Lord should take me before she got the chance. I lay down. Who knew if I would wake up again? But an angel woke me and urged me to eat. And sure enough, there was fresh bread and a jug of water on the stones next to me. I didn't realise how hungry I was and, when I had eaten, I fell asleep again. The same thing happened again, although this time the angel told me that I would need my strength for the journey. I wondered if I would have to go back and face Jezebel, or whether I was being taken somewhere else.

I didn't have to wait long to find out: my destination was Sinai. The mountain of God. It was the very place where our ancestor, Moses, had spoken with the Lord and seen His glory. I felt a kind of nervous excitement. What did this mean? Was I going to be allowed to see God too? Would He be pleased with me or annoyed that I had killed four hundred and fifty prophets on my own authority? I thought I was ready with answers but, although I had received strength for the journey, I was still pretty shattered.

"What are you doing here, Elijah?" God asked me, as I sat in a cave that I'd found. I was confused. Hadn't this journey been His idea? But I replied, "I have zealously served Almighty God. But the people of Israel have broken their covenant with You and killed all Your prophets. I am the only one left." I hadn't planned on saying that, but it was how I felt, and I was too tired and disillusioned to try to cover up my feelings.

"Go outside," God told me, and suddenly a mighty wind hit the mountain and swirled around it, throwing the rocks around like they were pieces of parchment. Then there was an earthquake that was so strong that the mountain shook. And this was followed by a scorching fire. I'd like to be able to say that God was showing His displeasure at the way that I had been treated. But God wasn't in any of these elements. Then I heard a gentle whisper – soft and soothing.

That was Almighty God, El Shaddai.

He asked me again what I was doing there. I was puzzled, but my reply hadn't changed, despite the pyrotechnic display I had just witnessed. Was I feeling sorry for myself? "I am the only prophet left," I whispered, "And now they want to kill me too." God didn't contradict, try to reason with or counsel me. He told me to go back the way I had come, to anoint two men as kings and Elisha, as a prophet, to replace me. I was not on my own. Not only was Elisha to continue the work after I had gone, but there were also seven thousand people in the land who had not bowed done to Baal or worshipped him. There was hope.

I met up with Ahab and Jezebel some time later. Ahab had taken a fancy to a vineyard owned by a man named Naboth and wanted to buy it from him. Naboth had refused because it was a family heirloom. Ahab had seemed to be prepared to accept the situation, but Jezebel said that she would get this vineyard for him. She did this by having Naboth falsely accused of treason and then stoned to death. Maybe this was revenge for the killing of Baal's prophets; maybe Jezebel didn't care that she was breaking the commandments of the God of Israel. Ahab should have known better though and God had a message for him because he had been unable to stand up to his wife. To his credit, and my complete surprise, Ahab seemed very subdued after this warning and seemed to show remorse for his sins. It didn't last long and he was later killed in battle. But maybe, for that short time, there was hope for him too.

I later brought the Word of the Lord to another king. He didn't know me, but he knew my role and calling by my robe of camel's hair and the belt around my waist – the robes of a prophet of the Lord.

That is my story. I finished the work that I was given to do and anointed Elisha, who will take over my work in bringing God's Word to the people and the people back to God. I will soon be taken into the presence of the God I have served for all these years. I hope that I have done my work faithfully and faithfully proclaimed that the Lord is God.

I wonder if people will remember that the Lord is God and put their trust in Him.

AS TOLD BY

Chapter 8
The Locust Muncher
As Told by John the Baptiser

My name is John. My father, Zechariah, was a priest and my mother, Elizabeth, was herself from a priestly line. They were good, devout people and worshipped God, but had no children. I imagine that must have been a great sadness to them.

You may be wondering how a man can introduce his parents as being childless. The fact was that they tried for many years to have children, reached an age when it would no longer be possible, and were then given their very own miracle. It happened like this:

Dad's priestly order was on duty in the temple. During their spell of duty, a priest would go into the Most Holy place where, it was believed, God lived. They would draw lots to determine who would have the privilege of going in to meet with God. Dad was chosen. While he was there, he had the most extraordinary encounter with an angel, who told him that God had heard his prayers and that he and his wife would have a son. Not only that but that

> *"he will go on before the Lord, in the spirit and power of Elijah,....to make ready a people prepared for the Lord"* (Luke 1:17).

All this must have been quite overwhelming. Firstly,

Dad had been chosen to go into the Holiest place. Then God sent an angel to meet with him and thirdly he was told that his dream was about to come true. My father asked how he could be certain that this would happen – after all, he and his wife were old. Now obviously, I didn't hear the tone of voice he used. Maybe there was an edge to it. Maybe he just didn't believe the message. Whatever it was, the angel seemed annoyed by his response. He reminded Dad that he was Gabriel, who stood in the presence of God and had been given that message by God Himself. Because Dad didn't believe his words, he would not be able to speak until I was born and the angel's words had indeed been fulfilled.

And it was so. When I was born, I was going to be called Zechariah after my father. But when the neighbours and family asked what my name should be, my mother said, "His name is John." There was no one in the family with that name, so they protested and asked Dad what he thought. He wrote on a tablet, "His name is John." He then immediately recovered his powers of speech and began praising God. He gave a prophecy about my future that I would be called, "the Prophet of the Most High" and would prepare the way for the Lord. News spread about this incident and it was clear that God was with me in a special way.

A few months later, one of Mum's relatives also gave birth to a boy, whom they called Jesus. I was told that I had already "met" this baby. His mother, Mary, went to visit my mother before I was born and, apparently, I moved as soon as I heard Mary's voice. Maybe that was an instinctive thing that I, somehow, recognised that she would give birth to a very important child. Maybe God spoke to me even before birth. As a child, I don't think I had the sense that Jesus was particularly special. He was kind, yes – loving, thoughtful, wise, very keen on the Scriptures and eager to learn about our faith and our ancestors. Yet there was nothing to make anyone believe that He might be God's Chosen One.

There had been whispers about his birth. Mary and Joseph hadn't been married, they said. Mary had been with someone else but claimed that God did it, they said. I can't imagine that would have happened. But anyway, to all intents and purposes, Joseph was Jesus' father. It didn't affect us or make much difference and we had an uneventful childhood until we were twelve – the year in which Jewish boys come of age. Being older, I naturally reached that milestone first and became a son of the Law. It was then that my parents felt I should know of the circumstances of my birth. They told me, too, that the angel had told my father that I would be great in God's sight. I had been filled with God's Spirit from birth, and my calling was to turn many people back to God.

This was all very overwhelming and, apart from the knowledge that God had important work for me to do, I wasn't sure what to make of it. Several months later, when Jesus was twelve, we went to Jerusalem to celebrate the Passover. Passover was an important feast, one which all Jewish men were required to observe. It was our first Passover as children of the

Law and it was a special time. There was some concern on the way home when Mary and Joseph lost Jesus and had to retrace their steps to look for Him. I heard that they found Him in the Temple and that He had said that He had to be in His Father's house. God's Temple: His Father's house?

It seemed that, in the year that we came of age, we both began to realise that we had a special calling on our lives. But from then on, our paths diverged. Jesus returned to live with His parents and I continued my education in the wilderness. I was there for many years. Yes, they were long and, at times, lonely. But the wilderness is a place of growth, discovery and discipline. I had to work out what God's words meant and how I was to go about the enormous task of turning people back to God. It's tough waiting, but when God calls us to a task, He first prepares us for it.

Some years later, God spoke to me and I knew it was time to leave the wilderness. I was called to go forth in the spirit of Elijah, so I don't think it was entirely coincidental that I was first seen wearing a tunic of camel hair with a leather belt around my waist. My message was one of repentance. It was harsh, but it needed to be. Centuries before, God had chosen the Hebrew people to be His people, but that had led many to believe that they could live how they liked. If they did wrong, they would be safe from punishment because they were God's chosen people. People began to take our holy God for granted and lived unwisely.

That belief was condemned by the prophets who sought to correct it, but not even a spell in exile had completely crushed it. My people would not be saved from God's judgement just because they were descendants of Abraham. They needed to realise that their sins had hurt God, to repent (or turn away from) those sins and then do something to show their willingness to lead a new life. That something meant being immersed under the murky waters of the Jordan River. I wasn't sure how this word would be received. God, through Moses, had given us the sacrificial system and instructions about how to atone for our sins. Penitent sinners weren't baptised. That was for non-Jews – unclean people – who wanted to convert to our faith. And yet, people responded to my message. Or rather, they responded to God.

Strangely, the religious leaders, whose job it was to teach about God, didn't like what I was doing. Maybe they thought that if there was to be any spiritual awakening, it should come through them and that God would work through the "proper channels." They demanded to know who I was and, to be fair, some of the crowd were probably wondering as well. So I told them, "I am not the Messiah." I was preparing the way for the Messiah and making sure God's people were ready to receive their Chosen One.   After four hundred years, during which time my people did not hear from God at all, I was the voice crying in the wilderness. The barren times were over; the spiritual drought ended. God was about to act. The One who came after me would baptise all in the waters of His life-giving Spirit.

And then I saw him.

Jesus.

I was shocked to see Him making His way towards me. My first thought was that there was a family problem. But then it hit me that this was God's Chosen One: my cousin, Jesus and the boy I grew up with. Then He, God's Chosen One, requested baptism, just like everyone else. I protested. The Chosen One didn't need to be baptised. If anything, He should have been baptising me. But Jesus said that it needed to be done to carry out all that God required. I didn't argue. I was glad that I hadn't. As I was bringing Jesus up out of the water, I saw a solitary, white dove, which circled and then landed on Jesus' head. Then I heard the Spirit, the Sprit who had been in me since birth, confirm that this was the One who would baptise others in His Holy Spirit.

That was my testimony. Jesus was the Messiah, the One who would usher in the Kingdom of God and baptise people in God's Holy Spirit. Jesus was the Lamb of God who would take away the sins of the world; just as the angel had foretold. Some of my disciples, who heard me say this, immediately went to Jesus and began to follow Him. This caused a few grumbles that Jesus was "poaching" my followers. But who could blame them? Not I. I didn't need to have hordes of fans or to be someone important. I was the friend who stood beside the bridegroom and rejoiced in his happiness. I had been sent to turn people back to God and my task would soon be done; Jesus' ministry was just beginning.

I didn't realise quite how soon my task would come to an end. Herod the Great had divided up his empire and appointed his sons as rulers. Galilee was ruled over by Herod Antipas who was married to Herodias, the daughter of his own half-brother. I had been sent to preach repentance and prepare the way for the Lord, but there was little sense in a nation that had turned back to God if its leaders, albeit Romans, were still in their sin and not ready to welcome God's Chosen One. Herod's marriage was an affront to us and against Jewish law. I told him so. I didn't expect this message to be popular or palatable. Though Herod was, at heart, Jewish and could have been expected to be awaiting the Jewish Messiah, he also had close ties with Rome and was heavily influenced by them. Besides, no one likes to be spotlighted for the wrong reasons. I was thrown into prison. After spending many years in the wide spaces of the wilderness, I was trapped in a dark, dank cell, almost certain what my final fate was to be. I still had a few disciples and, gradually, they brought me news of Jesus' ministry. All good stuff. But everyone knew the Messiah would be a military leader who would form an army, rally the faithful and drive out our enemies, the Romans. When would that start to happen? I had to ask,

> *"Are You the One who is to come, or should we expect someone else?"* (Luke 7:19)

My disciples were told to tell me what they could see

and hear: the blind were receiving their sight, the lame walking, the dead were raised and the Good News proclaimed. Jesus' words and actions spoke of a God who loved and cared for His people. The answer had been "yes" and "no." Jesus was surely "The One" – the signs and wonders showed that. But He was not the kind of Messiah we had been expecting: a warrior king who would declare war on our enemies. The Kingdom of God is founded on mercy, justice, kindness and love – not military might and violence.

And that is my story. My time here is short. Herod is a man who does rule by military might and violence. He will silence me and it will seem as though he has won, or that might is right. But God's will and purpose cannot be silenced. His Kingdom cannot be cancelled out. His Chosen One, of whom the prophets spoke, is Jesus and His rule is one of love, forgiveness mercy and peace.

I hope that Jesus will turn all people back to God so that they trust in His love and care, and that there will be peace.

Chapter 9
A Special Calling
As Told by Mary

My name is Mary. My husband's name was Joseph and he is from the lineage of King David. My story begins when Joseph and I were engaged to be married. Joseph was a bit older than me, but he was wise, patient and godly. I knew that he would take care of me and was looking forward to married life. I thought that we would have children and grow old together.

All that changed on the day that I saw the angel.

Oh, I know that might sound fantastic or farfetched. I wasn't sure myself what to make of this, even though many of God's people have met them. But that's how it was. There was suddenly an angel in front of me one day, telling me that I was favoured and that the Lord was with me. I didn't know what this meant, nor did I see any particular reason why God would favour me. The angel told me not to be afraid and that I was going to have a son. Well yes, Joseph and I had planned to have children one day, and one of them would probably be a boy.

The angel continued,

"He will be great and will be called the Son of the Most High. The Lord God will give him the throne

of his father David,...His kingdom will never end" (Luke 1:32–33).

OK, that was amazing. But why was he telling me this?

"You mean, I'm going to be pregnant before the wedding? That's not possible. How can I, a virgin, conceive?" The angel explained that the Holy Spirit would come to me, and I would be with child. Because of this, the child would be holy and be called the Son of God. Joseph wouldn't be involved.

I'm sorry...what?

The angel seemed to understand my confusion and reminded me that my cousin, Elizabeth, who was now too old to have children, was pregnant. He added that nothing was too difficult for God. Well, no, I don't suppose it is. God can do anything; that's what His name, El Shaddai, means. My head was still swimming. What a day this was turning out to be – what a shock, and privilege.

What would Joseph say? What about my parents? What would happen when people saw that I was with child, yet knew that we were still unmarried? How awesome and yet, terrifying. I didn't have answers. But I did know that this angel was from God and his message was real. So there was only one thing I could say,

"I am the Lord's servant. May your word to me be fulfilled" (Luke 1:38).

And, although Almighty God did not need my permission for anything, the angel seemed pleased at that response. Then he left me.

Still, in a daze, the first person I needed to tell was Joseph. But how would he react to the news that I was with child and he was not the father? He would think I had been with someone else. How was I going to convince him otherwise? I should have realised that God had it in hand. Joseph had had an angelic visitor of his own. He already knew about the baby and was assured that the child was from God. The angel told him that he should not be afraid to go ahead with his plans to marry me. How amazing, faithful and devoted was my betrothed! It required great strength, and love, to stand by me and to tell his critics, "This is God's child", and to face the scorn, mocking and pitying looks that accompanied such an answer.

Those next few months were far from easy, but soon the birth was only a few weeks away. Then Caesar decided to take a census, which meant that everyone had to register in their home town. As Joseph was from the tribe of Judah, that meant travelling to Bethlehem. Seriously? We had to travel to Bethlehem? Hadn't God already asked enough of me? Why would He allow this?

It was puzzling and frustrating. But there was no time to fret or try to work it out; we had to go. It was a long, uncomfortable journey and I longed to lie down. But, on arrival, we found the town was packed with those who needed to be there for the census.

They all needed somewhere to stay, and there was no room for us.

But...

Was it not enough that God wanted me to be an unmarried mother, and carry His Son? Couldn't He have at least arranged accommodation? Why did He have to make life so much harder? I was perplexed and disappointed. But I felt too tired and uncomfortable to dwell on such things. I just needed somewhere warm to stay and rest until the baby arrived.

And it was so. Our boy – our special, precious boy – was born. There was no lodging available for us so I wrapped Him snugly in strips of cloth and lay Him in a manger, (Luke 2:7). We had several visitors over the next few weeks, who also seemed to know that our boy was special and precious. The first was a group of shepherds, who had, themselves, seen angels and been told that the Messiah had been born. They came, marvelled and went away rejoicing. Next, we met Simeon, a devout man, and Anna, a prophetess, when we took Jesus to the temple to present Him to God. Simeon had been told by God that he would not die until he had seen the Messiah. When he saw us, he took Jesus in his arms, blessed us and said that he could die happy. He also made the strange statement that a sword would pierce my soul. I didn't know what that meant but supposed that it referred to the sorrow that I might feel one day when Jesus had grown up and left home. Anna also praised God when she saw Jesus and confirmed that he would be used by God in some way when he was older. Some time later, some Magi from a distant land also came to see and worship God. They brought many treasures, which was nice but rather puzzling. And then there was someone who didn't come to see Jesus – King Herod. Joseph had a warning from an angel that Herod wanted, in fact, to kill our son. So we gathered our things and fled to Egypt. That was a frightening, and puzzling, time. Herod appeared to think that our boy was a threat to him, in some way. We had to travel, secretly, to Egypt while hoping that if we lay low for a few weeks, we could then return. It was two years before we were able to go home.

Upon our return, we settled in Nazareth. We added to our family over the next few years, and the children were growing up. When Jesus was twelve, we went to the temple in Jerusalem to celebrate the feast of Passover and to mark His coming of age as an adult. We had made the journey before. All male Jews were required to go to the temple to celebrate the three major feasts, so there was a large crowd of us; each with the same purpose.

When the feast was over, we started out again for home. The women started out first, as was the custom. We walked more slowly, having our families to care for. Jesus wasn't travelling with me. I assumed He was with Joseph and the other adult men. What a shock I got when I found that He wasn't! No one in our group had seen Him either. By this time we had been travelling for a day and it was a long way back to Jerusalem. Yet, obviously, we had to go. We looked everywhere for Him. Eventually, we found Him in the temple, listening to the teachers. I asked Jesus where He had been – my tone no doubt sharpened by fear, anxiety and frustration. I'll never forget His reply,

"Why were you searching for Me? Didn't you know I had to be in My Father's house?" (Luke 2:49)

It was only much later that I began to understand what He had meant by that. I only later reflected on the fact that my boy knew who He was, and where He'd come from. In the meantime, we returned home.

The years passed, though we were so wrapped up in family life we scarcely noticed them. Joseph sadly died and Jesus became head of the family. I did worry about my children's futures, but more so with Jesus. Sometimes I saw Him in Joseph's workshop and wondered. Sawing and nailing wood was about as far away from inheriting the throne of David as it was possible to get. What was going to happen to Him? Had the angels made a mistake? I heard from Elizabeth that her son, John, had left the wilderness, was baptising people in the river Jordan and speaking of the One who would come after him. A short time later Jesus left our home; never to return.

During the following year, I heard many stories about my boy, all of which brought back memories. He taught in the Synagogue in Nazareth one Sabbath, and my mind went back to the earnest twelve-year-old sitting in the temple, asking questions, and listening. He told a paralysed man his sins were forgiven, and I recalled how his own name, Jesus, means "the Lord saves." A blind man referred to Him as the Son of David, and I remembered the angel's promise. On one occasion, word had reached us that Jesus was being mobbed wherever He went – so much so that He didn't even have time to eat! I can't remember whose idea it was, but the feeling was that the family needed to take Him in hand. Doing God's work is all very well, but looking after yourself is important too.

We went down to where He was, and I heard someone telling Him that His mother and brothers were outside. I was hurt by His comment that "anyone who does God's will is My brother and sister and mother." Had He forgotten His roots; had success turned His head? Was this what Simeon had meant when He'd said,

"And a sword will pierce your own soul too"? (Luke 2:35)

That was nothing compared with what was to come.

They say that you always remember what you were doing at the big moments in life. But I had no idea where I was when I heard that my eldest had been arrested. It had to be a mistake, obviously. Jesus never hurt anyone – quite the opposite. He was popular, kind and well thought of. He talked and taught about God in a way that no one else ever had and had natural authority. Were the religious leaders trying to warn Him or frighten Him? If so, why would they resort to false witnesses and illegal trials? I was afraid for Him, and frantic to help.

It was all over and I was standing at the bottom of a hill, watching my firstborn dying in agony.

Simeon had been wrong. The sharp sword of sorrow did not pierce my soul, it cut it to shreds. I had never felt such pain and knew that I would never heal. My sister, a couple of other women and one of the disciples were there with me, but I hardly noticed. It was just me and Jesus – as it had been in the beginning. Somewhere, inside my head, a multitude of questions were fighting to get out. Why the angelic protection at birth? Why the adoration and promises of greatness? Why the hurried escape to Egypt if it was all going to end like this? I could see that He was trying to speak. What would He say? "I love you" maybe? "I'm sorry"? What can a person say when they are blinded by pain, slowly suffocating, every breath, torture? Instead, He told His disciple that I was his mother, and he, was my son. At the very end, in the pain and dust of broken dreams, my boy's thoughts were for His mother. Then Jesus took one last, gasping breath and was silent.

Somehow, I got back to John's house that evening. The next day was the Sabbath, but I don't think anyone noticed; it wasn't very restful. The morning after that, while it was still dark, some of us took some spices and made our way to the tomb. We were eager to get there, yet we weren't. Anointing the body would make it all so final. But it was the final thing I could do for my son, "Wrap him snugly in strips of cloth."

But we were in for a shock.

The stone that had been covering the tomb had been rolled away, and there was nothing, or no-one, inside. Lost in my thoughts and wondering how much more grief I could bear, I hardly noticed when two men appeared beside us. Indeed, maybe I wouldn't have done but for the fact that their clothes gleamed like lightning. Angels! They had announced Jesus' birth, now they were announcing – what? "Why do you look for the living among the dead?" they asked us. "He is not here, for He has risen."

We remembered, then, that Jesus Himself had told us this; He had known that it would happen. We rushed off to tell His disciples; who, needless to say, didn't believe us.

That is my story. I had the awesome privilege of bringing Jesus, the Chosen One, into this world. I didn't know of God's plan for Him, but God did. That plan, inexplicably, included suffering and death, but also resurrection. Jesus, my son, really had been dead, and now really was alive again.

I wonder whether He will now receive the throne of His ancestor, David.

AS TOLD BY

Chapter 10

The Forgotten Ones

As Told by Two Female Disciples

The Samaritan Woman

My name is—well, I don't suppose my name matters as I am a woman. A Samaritan woman.

Samaritans and Jews don't get on. I mean, we really don't get on. It has something to do with when the country was divided after Solomon died, I think. Those Northerners always felt that they were better than us because they had the temple and worshipped in Jerusalem. We didn't have a temple and worshipped in Samaria. It's horrible to be excluded, though I'm used to that.

It's one thing to be excluded by Jews, it's quite another to feel excluded by your own people. But having been rejected, or abandoned, by five husbands, tongues have inevitably started to wag. What is it about me that causes everyone to leave me? For this reason, I usually go out around noon because it's less likely that anyone will see me. Arriving at Jacob's well one day, however, I was surprised to see someone already there – a Jewish man. I was even more surprised when He asked me for a drink of water.

"You are a Jew and I am a Samaritan woman," I said, "How can You ask me for a drink?" (John 4:9)

I must confess, I didn't entirely understand His statement that He could give me living water. But it sounded good to me: having running water would mean that I need never come to this well again. So I asked Him if He would give this water to me. "Go, call your husband and come back," this man instructed me. I didn't know what my marital status had to do with anything, nor why it was His business. But I was unable to voice those thoughts and heard myself confessing, "I don't have a husband." The man agreed. He knew of my past, and that I was now living with someone I was not married to. This was getting too close for comfort. This man had come for a drink of water. Why start dragging my private life into it? It seemed that He was a prophet or a man of God. Holy men didn't usually have anything to do with the likes of me, but here was one, standing in front of me. So I asked Him something I had always wanted to know. Where was the correct place to worship God: in Samaria or in Jerusalem? He didn't give me an answer or, at least, the short answer seemed to be "neither." His longer answer talked about not knowing whom we worshipped and that salvation would come from the Jews. I don't mind admitting that I was a bit out of my depth by now, so I think I said that I expected the Messiah would be able to explain this to us when He got here.

Then he told me, "I am the Messiah."

What? This man was claiming to be the Christ. He had used God's own name, "I AM." It was the special name that had been revealed to Moses. This man had revealed this to me! What was going on?

At this point, a few other men turned up. It seemed that they knew this man of God quite well and called Him, Jesus. I could see the shock and disdain on their faces when they realised who He had been talking to; sadly, I was used to that. Strangely though, no one questioned Him about it. I was still trying to process everything. I had been talking to a man of God, who seemed to know all the secrets of my life, yet He didn't judge me. He had also told me that He was the Christ. Was He mad? Was He an imposter?

True, I hadn't understood all of our conversation, but He seemed to be neither. Would an imposter have stopped by a well in enemy territory and spoken to a woman? Wouldn't an imposter have judged me for my sins, or found a way to exploit me? Was it possible that this man was who He said He was? I ran back to my village.

> *"Come and see a man who told me everything I ever did!" I said to them. "Could this be the Messiah?"* (John 4:29)

Surprisingly, people listened to me and then went to see for themselves. As a result, Jesus stayed in Samaria for two more days – long enough for almost everyone to hear His teaching and His message and put their faith in Him.

I wonder how many others will do so.

AS TOLD BY

Mary Magdalene

My name is Mary and I am from the town of Magdala. I had a difficult upbringing and life. The details don't matter anymore. Suffice it to say that everybody has demons: character traits, weaknesses, destructive habits, whatever you like to call them. I certainly had them, and they were making my life miserable. Then I met Jesus of Nazareth, and He delivered me from them. God still saves people from slavery to sin, despair, past hurts, bad habits and those things which torment us; and I couldn't thank Him enough. I began to follow Him after that. Well, wouldn't you want to be with someone who loved you unconditionally and wanted the best for you? I wasn't one of Jesus' closest followers. I reckon He had to choose only men for that role because women had such a bad press. But I also wanted to be where He was and to learn from Him. And learn I did.

He was an amazing teacher and spoke about God in a new and exciting way. After centuries of only being able to approach God through prophets, Jesus said that we could pray to the God of Abraham, Isaac and Jacob directly without an intermediary. He taught us that God is not frightening, stern or aloof, nor someone who has to be appeased. He taught us that El Shaddai is our Father. In fact, He said we should use the word "Abba" (which is very informal).

Our leaders tell us that we can only form a synagogue, which is a place of worship, if there are ten men present. Jesus taught that God is present if only two or three are gathered in His name. He taught that God cared for even sparrows who fell out of trees, and all the more for humans, who are much more valuable. Jesus lived out his teachings too. He ate and drank with tax collectors, sinners and even gentiles. He touched those who were ritually unclean – such as lepers or a woman who was bleeding. He healed them so that they were well and no longer ritually unclean. He even brought the dead back to life. As someone said,

"He has done everything well" (Mark 7:37).

It must be said though that the religious leaders didn't like some of his teachings and the way that He helped ordinary people to come to God. That, they believed, was their territory. I don't know what I expected in years to come; I hadn't thought that far ahead. I suppose I expected that Jesus would continue to teach and heal. I hoped that, in time, the religious leaders would come to accept Jesus, maybe even embrace His teachings about God.

I didn't expect them to have Him killed.

Jesus had gone to Jerusalem. He had travelled around a lot in three and a half years, but this time His journey to Jerusalem seemed more purposeful. Some tried to suggest that He should stay away; other areas of the country, although occupied by the Romans, were safer. But He seemed determined. He was probably right. We were coming up to Passover – a very busy time. Jews from all over the area, and maybe beyond, would be headed for the city and the temple. Surely Jesus would be safe walking in, among a crowd of thousands? But Jesus didn't walk into the city. He rode in on a donkey. It was harmless enough at the time, and it was also evident that He was popular with the crowd. Yet a few days later, they arrested Him and then sentenced Him to be crucified.

It was a dreadful day; I'll never forget it. I, and a few others, followed Him as He carried His cross. We then stood at the foot of it and watched Him die. We were allowed to be there – we were only women and didn't pose a threat to anyone. I wanted to be there for Him. He had taken away my darkness. If I could lighten His, even a little, that's what I would do. One of His followers, Joseph, decided to ask for His body so that it could be buried in a new tomb, rather than be flung into a common grave with other criminals. But there was no time to embalm the body before the Sabbath. I wondered if some of us might go to embalm His body when the Sabbath was over.

And it was so. After the Sabbath, we hurried to the tomb, as early as we could – we hadn't slept, anyway. We just wanted to do one last thing for Someone who had meant so much to us: a thoughtful, kind, gentle man who had accepted us as we were. He had dignified us as women, and the least we could do was to give Him dignity in death. It only struck us on the journey that His tomb had been sealed with a heavy stone, and no one could roll it away for us. As it turned out, we didn't have that problem. I thought that Joseph or one of the twelve had moved it and had gone inside to embalm the body. I don't know whether we were pleased at not having to roll it away, or annoyed that we'd been denied one last chance to show that we cared. We went inside.

We got a real shock when we saw that the body wasn't there.

Was this the Romans playing mind games? Were they trying to lure His followers out of hiding? The others went away; it's not possible to anoint something that has disappeared. But I was too upset. It wasn't fair. Jesus couldn't hurt anyone now (not that He would ever have done so anyway). Why couldn't they give Him some dignity in death? Lost in my thoughts and grief, I almost missed the gardener, who was standing close by. He asked me why I was crying, and I managed to say that someone had moved, or stolen, my Lord's body.

> *"Sir," I said, "If you have carried Him away, tell me where you have put Him, and I will get Him"* (John 20:15).

"Mary," the man replied, with a smile.

Jesus!

But...we saw Him die! Had we been mistaken? How? When? Why? I didn't know. I just knew that He was standing in front of me, smiling. I rushed to hold onto Him, to have that assurance that He was real. He told me not to do so, but to go and tell His brothers that He was alive. They didn't believe me, of course – I'm only a woman. But Peter and John rushed off to the tomb though and found it was as I had said.

And that is my story – though it's not the end of my story. I was once a broken, tormented woman. I was invisible because of my gender; cast aside due to the demons within me. Jesus noticed me, healed me, affirmed me and gave me a purpose in life. I don't yet know why His own life was taken from Him. I suspect those images of crucifixion will linger for some time. But He is alive again.

I've often wondered: Why me? Was it luck, or a coincidence that I was in the garden at the time? Was this some kind of reward for our loyalty in following Jesus all the way to the cross? And I couldn't help thinking about Eve, the first woman, whose relationship with God was broken because she was deceived, and ultimately disobedient.

She lost her Lord in a garden. I found my Lord in a garden.

Could it be that I was somehow chosen to be the first witness to the resurrection? It wasn't because of anything I had done, but because our Lord chose to restore women, as well as all things.

Chapter 11
The Son of Thunder
As Told by John

My name is John. My father's name is Zebedee and I have a brother, James. We are fishermen.

It's interesting in which direction life takes us sometimes – a chance encounter, an unexpected meeting or conversation, and everything changes. Such was the case when we met Jesus. I had seen Him around, this young preacher, but didn't know much about Him. He seemed to be OK. He certainly drew the crowds and there were stories of sick people being made well after this man simply prayed to God. One day, Simon and a few others were cleaning their nets after a long and fruitless night when Jesus came by, asked them if He could use a boat, got into it and started teaching. This man spoke about God in a new way; almost as though He had met Him personally.

He finished speaking and the crowds began to drift away. The men were about to walk away too. They hadn't caught anything all night – it's like that sometimes. Jesus then told Simon to go out where it was deeper and let down His nets. I couldn't see Simon's expression but I expected he was a tad irritated. Jesus seemed to be a gifted teacher but clearly knew little about our trade. But Simon did as He said. James and I were in a nearby boat with our father when we heard the shout. There were fish everywhere! We rushed to help with the nets before the boat sank. Amazing. This wasn't just luck. This was the kind of miracle that God used to do. What did it mean?

Jesus said that, from then on, we fishermen would be fishers of men (people) and invited us to follow Him. We had no idea what that meant, we just wanted to be with Him and learn more. James and I went too, leaving Dad to clean our boat on his own. We expected to receive a mouthful from him later that evening. We never returned home.

So who was this carpenter's son from Nazareth: a quiet, almost unassuming man who could conjure up fish from nowhere? A man with such presence and authority that people dropped everything (literally) to do as He asked? I've been pondering that question for most of my life and I'm still not sure that there is a straightforward answer. Firstly, there were the miracles. We saw some amazing sights during our time with Jesus: blind men regained their sight and people who had never walked skipped around like young lambs. Jesus healed single individuals, like Peter's mother-in-law; quiet miracles that would have been missed by many. He publicly healed crowds – so many, that they were lining up at the town gate (Mark 1:33) or spilling out of a house (Mark 2:1–4). He risked becoming ritually unclean by associating with and touching, lepers, the demon-possessed, dead people and a woman who had been bleeding for many years. He healed some from a distance; He didn't even need to see them. Jesus was popular.

Men, women and children had their lives changed by meeting Him and spending time with Him. He welcomed all – and I mean all – and told them that the God who had made them also loved them and wanted them to know Him. Jesus didn't only talk about God with the religious leaders, nor did He tell the Good News only to "nice" people.

It was this determination to treat people as individuals, equally loved by God, that led Him into conflict with some of the religious teachers. It caused a few raised eyebrows amongst His followers too if I'm honest. Jesus gained a bit of a reputation for eating with tax collectors; those Jewish traitors who collected taxes on behalf of the Romans and took enough to line their own pockets too. One of them, Levi (or Matthew), even became one of our group of disciples. Jesus healed a servant belonging to a Roman centurion. A Roman – those infidels who had invaded the country and sought to conquer and subdue God's own people. Jesus welcomed, healed and treated them as individuals.

And Samaritans too. On one occasion we were going through Samaria (I don't know why; Jews and Samaritans don't get on.). Jesus saw a woman by a well, talked with her, told her that He was the Messiah and were invited to stay in the town for two days. Another time, they wouldn't even let us into the area because we were heading for Jerusalem. I may have got a bit over-enthusiastic at that point and wanted to call fire down from heaven to destroy them. I'd like to think that I was zealous, like Elijah, but maybe I was showing what a son of thunder looked like. Anyway, Jesus wasn't happy with me. He later told us a parable where a badly injured man was cared for by...yes, you've guessed it, a Samaritan. He told us to go and do likewise.

Why was Jesus spending so much time teaching and healing those who hated us? Yet even when He was showing compassion to His own people, it didn't meet with everyone's approval. He once healed a man with a shrivelled hand, causing him great joy and the religious leaders great displeasure, because He had chosen to perform this act of compassion on the Sabbath. So Jesus' actions brought great joy, healing, restoration and hope to many. But they also brought upset and division.

Then there was His teaching. Jesus taught with an authority quite unlike that of our teachers of the law. He talked about God as no one ever had before. He always called God "Father." The word He used, in fact, was "Abba" (which is an intimate, informal term). He taught us to use that name too. Imagine that! The prophets had known God as "El Shaddai" or Almighty God ("Adonai", which means Lord, or "I AM" which was the special name God revealed to Moses). Yet Jesus of Nazareth told us that we could call God "Daddy."

It seemed that almost any occasion, any miracle or even confrontation could become a teaching opportunity. One time, His teaching drew a crowd of more than five thousand — they were there for hours. Ever compassionate, Jesus wondered where we would find enough food to feed the crowd. Ever practical, Philip pointed out that it would cost a lot of money to be able to buy that food. So Jesus gave them their miracle and fed them with a few bread rolls and a couple of fish. Then He used the occasion to talk about Moses giving their ancestors manna from heaven while He, who had come from heaven, was the Bread of Life.

He once healed a man who had been born blind. That's right. We watched as this man regained his sight, seeing the beauty of the world and his parents' faces for the first time. Nobody could believe it; they didn't even think that it was the same man and there was much excited chatter. The Pharisees, however, didn't like this at all. Once again, they ignored the God-given miracle and focused on the fact that Jesus had healed on the Sabbath. They questioned the man about what had happened, and his parents about whether he really had been blind. Then they, the nation's religious leaders and teachers, threw the man out of the synagogue because he had dared to suggest that Jesus might have been from God.

After that, Jesus took the opportunity to speak about spiritual blindness and also about false teachers. He commented that those who were bad shepherds did not truly know, or care for, the sheep in their charge. Any sign of a wolf, or danger, and they ran off. A good shepherd, however, knew his sheep by name; in fact, the sheep responded only to his voice. If the point wasn't clear enough, Jesus stated that He was the Good Shepherd and, unlike the bad shepherd, He had come to bring fullness of life.

Another time, Jesus' teaching seemed to precede the miracle. We had occasionally enjoyed the hospitality of two sisters, Mary and Martha (though I think Martha was the real hostess). They had a brother, Lazarus, who became gravely ill one day. Naturally, his sisters sent word to Jesus. But unfortunately, we were out of the area. When we returned, Lazarus had died. Some of us were puzzled by this. We knew what the sisters didn't — Jesus had not immediately set out to return when He heard the news of Lazarus' illness. We could not work out why. Jesus spoke to both Martha and Mary about the afterlife, the resurrection and so on. Martha expressed a belief that her brother would rise again on the last day. How that was going to immediately help her, goodness only knows. Jesus then announced that He was the resurrection and the life and that no one who believed in Him would die. This was minutes before Lazarus walked out of the tomb.

Yes, I know, but he really did! We had all heard the story of Elijah, one of our great prophets, who prayed to God and brought a widow's son back to life. We had no reason to doubt that story, but it had been many years before, in a different age. This was real, it was happening now, in front of us. Miracles and teaching. Teaching and miracles. Both were extraordinary. This was an extraordinary time.

Were the miracles to show us that God had the power to help us? Were there miracles to show us He cared about us? Was Jesus able to do them because He had been given this power? Was Jesus able to talk about God because He was especially close to, or been sent by, God? How else would He have known so much about Him?

"I AM the bread of life..."

"I AM the Good Shepherd..."

"I AM the resurrection and the life..."

Oh, my! There was that name again; the name that Almighty God revealed to Moses. Surely, Jesus of Nazareth could not use God's own name? Blasphemy is so very serious. The commandments say that God will not leave unpunished anyone who misuses His name (Exodus 20:7). Yet Jesus received no punishment.

If we thought about the future at all, I think we assumed that this would go on for many years; maybe until everyone had heard about God and seen evidence of His love and care. Maybe, even, the country would begin to turn back to God and ask Him to save us from this Roman occupation. Just think: Jesus could have been the one to do that and we could have been there, with Him, at the start of the revolution.

Jesus was so popular that he would have had a great following. It was about this time that He began to talk about His death.

I'm sorry, what?

Jesus was about the same age as some of us, and younger than others. He was doing important work: God's work. Hadn't He told the Samaritan woman, and Simon Peter, that He was the Messiah? Well, everyone knows the Messiah won't die. How was it that someone who was so popular, who had restored so many people and spoken of life — the life that He could give to others — could talk about His own violent death?

Yet He did.

He would, He said, be betrayed by those He had helped. He said He'd be arrested, beaten and then crucified. His life would be brutally cut short.

And it was so. And our dreams, hopes, joys — all that we had learnt and the wonders we had seen — died with Him. It was the end. It was all over, and nothing made sense.

All those people who were healed, restored, given a new life, even a second chance of life: What had been the point? The One who had restored that life could not save His own. What a miserable few days we had, shut up in an upper room. We were safe due to the locks on the doors; imprisoned by our fear, our sadness, our "what ifs."

Then Mary knocked at the door; breathless, face flushed, words tumbling over themselves, "

They have taken the Lord's body out of the tomb, and we don't know where they have put Him!" (John 20:2)

Peter and I ran out, straight to the tomb. He, of course, went in immediately; I held back. But we both saw the grave clothes, with the head cloth rolled up, separately. If the Romans had taken His body away, they would have picked it up, not unwrapped Him first and then rolled the grave clothes up again. Could it be? Mary later told us the full story. She had mistaken Him for the gardener. She thought that He might have seen something and begged to be told where her Lord's body was. She recognised Jesus after He called her by name.

This is not the end of my story. I could tell you of Pentecost and the awesome power of the Spirit which rested on us as tongues of fire. There seemed to be flames coming from us. We weren't even singed, but we were empowered to go out and proclaim the Good News. I could tell you of the crippled man who was healed, the privilege of telling people about Jesus and the opposition we endured for doing so. Maybe I will one day, but maybe not. Because this isn't about me. My life was, is and has been closely bound up with Jesus since the day that we were called.

I have written this,

> *"so that you may believe that Jesus is the Messiah, the Son of God and that by believing, you may have life in His name"* (John 20:31).

He is my purpose for writing and for living.

I pray that others may come to know and to trust in Him.

AS TOLD BY

Chapter 12
The Jesus Hater
As Told by Paul

My name is Saul. I am a Hebrew from the tribe of Benjamin. I also have Roman citizenship – as did my parents. I was born in Tarsus in Cilicia, and we later moved to Jerusalem. My faith, the faith of our forefathers – Abraham, Isaac and Jacob – was very important to me. I studied hard under Gamaliel and became a Pharisee.

My people have, for many years, been awaiting the coming of a Messiah: someone who would save us from our enemies and bring in the kingdom of God. Several charlatans had claimed that they were "The One", but none of them proved to be so. The latest person to have made this claim was a peasant carpenter-teacher, known as Jesus of Nazareth. True, He did do many good things and helped people. He also taught in a way that was lapped up by His followers and the uneducated people of Israel. Shockingly, a few of my fellow Pharisees were taken in by this nonsense. Most saw through Him, however, and He was put to death for His blasphemous lies. Had it been left to the Jews we would have stoned Him to death, as our law demanded. But the country was under Roman occupation and we needed to convince the Roman authorities to do it for us. That resulted in crucifixion.

But the method didn't really matter. Jesus of Nazareth was dead, that was that and it surely wouldn't be too long before His followers and hangers-on dispersed and went their own ways. Except, they didn't.

Three days after Jesus' death, I heard that His followers were spreading stories that He was alive again. Not only that, but they were also proclaiming Him as the Messiah, or Christ. Well, that was a false claim and I wasn't standing for it. I began to imprison some of the worst offenders. I have written elsewhere[3] of how Jesus met with me on the road to Damascus and called me to proclaim His name to the Gentiles. I was blinded for three days then my sight was restored – in more ways than one. I had thought I was persecuting the followers of the Way. I was, in fact, persecuting the Lord Himself: Jesus. It was He who had appeared to me, filled me with His Spirit and was now calling me to take the Good News to the Gentiles.

Before that could happen, though, I needed to think about this new revelation. I had to know what I believed, and why, if I were to have any chance of explaining it to others; whether Gentiles or Jews. The Pharisees and teachers of the law had been so sure that Jesus was not the Messiah. If He was, then our Scriptures and our prophets must surely have foretold this. Why did they not know what was written? Why did I not know? I decided to start from the beginning.

The first Messianic prophecy in the Bible can be

found in the first book of the Bible. After the serpent tempted Eve, God told it that one day it would be defeated, crushed, by the woman's descendent. That probably didn't make much sense to Eve, at the time. But, over the years, the serpent in the garden came to be identified with the devil: Beelzebub, Satan, the evil one. Only someone greater than the devil could crush the devil. Only God is greater than the devil. Yet the Messiah would also be a descendant of Eve's. This prophecy showed that God's Chosen One would be both human and divine.

Unknown to him, Abraham was given a prophecy about the Chosen One, when he was told that all the families of the earth would be blessed through him. Later, God repeated the promise that Abraham's descendants would become as numerous as the stars in the sky. The Chosen One would be a descendant of Abraham, who would restore the blessings of Eden.

Years later, Abraham's grandson, Jacob, blessed his twelve sons and said that the sceptre would not depart from Judah nor the ruler's staff from his descendants

> *"until the coming of the One to whom it belongs"* (Genesis 49:10).

The word translated as "One to whom it belongs" is "Shiloh" – another name for the Messiah. This was a prophecy that the Messiah would be a descendant of the tribe of Judah. David had been a king after God's heart. He wasn't perfect, but when he did wrong, he repented, sought God again and continued to follow. He put God first and trusted Him. David had wanted to build a house, or Temple, for God. It wasn't to be. God said that He would build a house for David; a dynasty of kings. God promised that David's house and his kingdom would continue for all time, and his throne would be secure forever (2 Samuel 7:16). Many years after this, God promised that He would make a righteous descendant (the Hebrew word means "branch") sprout from David's line (Jeremiah 33:15). The prophet Zechariah also spoke of this.

I found further prophecies about the Messiah in our Scriptures. Isaiah told us that a virgin would conceive and bear a son and that He would be called

"Immanuel" (Isaiah 7:14).

He also told us that the child to be born would be called "Wonderful Counsellor, Almighty God, Prince of Peace" and that He would rule from the throne of His father, David. Jewish tradition says that the Messiah will be called by eight names, including, "Wonderful Counsellor" and "Eternal Father of Peace." Despite this, Isaiah says, He will also be a

"man of sorrows acquainted with the deepest grief" (Isaiah 53:3)

and would be

"crushed for our sins" (Isaiah 53:5).

This was a surprise to me. We had always understood that the Messiah would be a great military leader who could not die. How had I not understood this before?

According to our prophets, then, God's Chosen One would be both human and divine, a descendant of Abraham and Jacob, from the tribe of Judah and a descendant of David. He would be called Wonderful Counsellor and Almighty God (El Shaddai), but He would also be rejected and suffer great pain for our sins. What has all this got to do with Jesus?

Although I had no intention of believing in Jesus before I met Him on the Damascus road, I did know a little about Him. It pays to know your enemy! I had been prepared to thoroughly oppose Him and everything that He stood for, but I soon learned that He was a Jew; circumcised and became a child of the law when He was twelve. He was someone who visited the temple and synagogues and, mostly, kept the Jewish feasts. He also read from, quoted and had learnt our Scriptures. He referred to people such as Abraham, David, Elijah and Moses. He was, by all appearances, an ordinary human being. I had also heard some of the whispers about His birth; how Mary claimed that she had not been with Joseph, but that it was God who made her pregnant. I could have dismissed the claims of a teenage girl, who was facing death by stoning due to her adultery, had it not been for the fact that Joseph, a good Jew with a good ancestry, said the same thing. He was prepared to stand by Mary and bring the boy up as his own. The angel had told Mary that her son would be given the throne of David, and hailed as "Wonderful Counsellor, Mighty God"; some of the names given to the Messiah. If it was true that Jesus was born of a virgin, then He was both human and divine. This goes back to the Garden of Eden and the prophecy that a descendant of Eve would crush the serpent's head.

It also seemed to me that several of these heroes of our faith had, unknowingly, pointed to and taught about Jesus. Adam had disobeyed the One who made him. As a result, mankind became separated from God. Sin, sickness and death came into the world. Jesus obeyed God perfectly, healed people from illness and, by His death and resurrection, forgiveness, hope and reconciliation with God are possible. Abraham was commanded to sacrifice His son, the child of the promise, as a sacrifice to God. He said to Isaac, "God Himself will provide a lamb for the burnt offering, my son." Centuries later, God Himself sent His Son to be an offering for the sins of the world. A ram died in Isaac's place; Jesus, the Lamb of God, died in ours. Moses had been called by God to lead the Hebrew slaves out of Egypt: a place of suffering, tyranny and death. He led them through the wilderness to God's holy mountain where they received His commandments and became His people. Much later, they entered the Promised Land. By His death, Jesus rescued us from slavery to sin and spiritual death, which is eternal separation from God. Not only did Jesus teach God's Word, but He is also the Word of God. After His ascension, Jesus sent His Spirit who lives in His followers today, to give us life, peace, hope and assurance that we belong to Almighty God (El Shaddai) and are His children.

David had been a young shepherd boy – an unlikely candidate for a king. Yet God had chosen and anointed him. Though far from perfect, God referred to David as "a man after My own heart" and made a promise to him that one of his descendants would always be on the throne. Jesus was descended from King David. Born to an unmarried girl, Mary, and growing up as a carpenter's son, He seemed an unlikely candidate for a Messiah. Yet an angel had said, before His birth, that He would be called "Wonderful Counsellor, Almighty God" (El Shaddai) and that His kingdom would never end. Elijah was a great prophet, who had brought people back to God and destroyed the worshippers of Baal. It was widely believed that, before the Messiah came, Elijah would reappear to announce His coming. John the Baptist was sent "in the spirit and power of Elijah" to turn people back to God and prepare the way for the Lord. Finally, Jesus, the Word, God's final Word, was born, lived among us and fulfilled those prophecies. Those who believe and trust in Him and His love have now come full circle – reconciled to God and walking in fellowship with Him just as Adam had once been.

And that is God's story. I had been a Pharisee from the tribe of Benjamin; very zealous for the law and passionate about the Hebrew Scriptures and faith. I had hated, and persecuted, the followers of Jesus and tried to stamp out this heretical sect who followed a false Messiah. I was the least likely candidate to be called to take the Good News of

Jesus, the Messiah, to others. Yet how could I do anything else after Jesus, whom my fellow Pharisees had seen die, appeared to me to tell me that He, the Lord, was alive and had chosen me to be His follower? If God had brought Jesus back from the dead, that could only mean that God approved of Jesus and that He had been who He had claimed to be. God wouldn't have raised a deluded, blasphemous man to life. Neither was it only His closest followers who had claimed that He was alive again. Jesus had appeared to over five hundred people before He appeared to me.

And all of this had been foretold, years before. Jesus' ancestry, His birth, life, ministry, betrayal and resurrection had all been foretold by our prophets and people of faith. It had all been there in our Scriptures. Yet it had meant little to me until the day when I met Jesus of Nazareth.

My life will end one day, maybe quite soon; yet it won't. Eternal life doesn't start when we die. Eternal life starts when we believe in the One who came to give life. I have had the joy of serving my Lord for many years and it was an honour, even with all the hardships and suffering.

I hope, and pray, that others will realise that the God who made them loves them. I hope they will come to know, and follow Jesus – the second Adam, descendant of Judah, Son of David, the Messiah – who has made all things new.

Conclusion

The Bible is a difficult book.

It's best not to start reading it from the beginning. It's difficult to know how to read it at all. For example, is it true? Must we believe every written word? Does all its teaching apply to us? Can we even trust those who wrote it? Then there is the content. It gives details of violence, war, incest, rape and other dubious behaviour. Surely these are not examples that we should be following. It contains genealogies and detailed instructions for the building of the Jewish temple – later destroyed. Surely these are not relevant to us. It contains difficult passages that we would rather not consider and don't know if we can accept.

The Bible is an amazing book! It's actually made up of sixty-six books, each with a different style and genre, of writing: historical, poetic, biographical and so on. It was written over many years by people from different countries, cultures and walks of life: kings, judges, fishermen and learned scholars. Yet there is a harmony about it. The thread running through it is that of God's love, His ways, His will and His desire to have a relationship with those whom He created. Words spoken by folk in the Old Testament are repeated, echoed and lived out hundreds of years later, by folk in the New. The Bible records events from long ago but contains words of comfort, hope, blessing and love which are relevant and have helped thousands today. Its stories of life, human nature and human predicaments resonate with us.

A theme running through the Old Testament is that of a Messiah, or deliverer; one who would come, put all things right and usher in God's kingdom. In the New Testament, this person is revealed as Jesus. The Gospels describe His life, ministry and death, and the Epistles show how His followers put His teaching into practice.

The Bible is a book of stories about people. Human nature is much the same now as it always has been. The Bible does not skip over the nasty bits, giving only the sanitised version, the stories about nice, faithful, pious people or the happily ever after endings. Sometimes the nicest people mess up; sometimes the worst people – those we might write off as hopeless – are accepted, called by God, and become His people. 'As Told By' has introduced you to some of these characters: widows, fishermen, a shepherd boy, murderers, liars. These are all human beings with characteristics, gifts, flaws and stories just like us. I hope you enjoyed it and are inspired to read and learn more about God's Word.

About the Author

Gill Taggart is a full-time volunteer and a lay preacher in the Methodist Church. She likes to use the creative arts in leading worship and is interested that many of these arts are also therapies. She enjoys crafts, gardening and music, and lives in Cheshire with two cats and her husband.

AS TOLD BY

Notes

[1] As in "The apple on the tree wasn't the problem; it was the pair on the ground" (Source unknown).

[2] In the NIV the place Harran is spelled this way to differentiate it from the man's name "Haran." Other translations use the latter spelling for both.

[3] Gill Taggart. 2023. 'Restored, Recycled, Remade.' PublishU. See chapter 12, 'Saul's Story'.

AS TOLD BY

About PublishU

PublishU is transforming the world of publishing.

PublishU has developed a new and unique approach to publishing books, offering a three-step guided journey to becoming a globally published author!

We enable hundreds of people a year to write their book within 100-days, publish their book in 100-days and launch their book over 100-days to impact tens of thousands of people worldwide.

The journey is transformative, one author said,

"I never thought I would be able to write a book, let alone in 100 days... now I'm asking myself what else have I told myself that can't be done that actually can?'"

To find out more visit
www.PublishU.com

AS TOLD BY

Printed in Great Britain
by Amazon